stepping in, stepping out:

creating stepfamily rhythm

Joshua M. Gold

AMERICAN COUNSELING
ASSOCIATION
6101 Stevenson Avenue, Suite 600
Alexandria, VA 22304
counseling.org

stepping in, stepping out:
creating stepfamily rhythm

10 9 8 7 6 5 4 3 2 1

American Counseling Association
6101 Stevenson Avenue, Suite 600
Alexandria, VA 22304

Associate Publisher   Carolyn C. Baker

Digital and Print Development Editor   Nancy Driver

Production Manager   Bonny E. Gaston

Copy Editor   Ida Audeh

Text and cover design by Bonny E. Gaston

Library of Congress Cataloging-in-Publication Data
Gold, Joshua M. (Joshua Mark)
    Stepping in, stepping out: creating stepfamily rhythm/Joshua Gold.
        pages cm
    Includes bibliographical references and index.
    ISBN 978-1-55620-331-2 (pbk.: alk. paper)   1. Stepfamilies.   2. Family counseling.   I. Title.
    HQ759.92.G65 2016
    306.874'7—dc23   2015023361

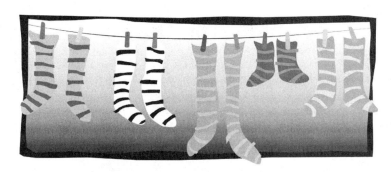

Contents

Chapter 9

Chapter 10

Preface

In the 1970s, U.S. viewers watched as *The Brady Bunch* (Schwartz, 1969–1974) homogenized two families into a perfectly blended home, as if nothing in the world was unusual or in any way challenging about the circumstances. In 30-minute sequences, siblings resolved benign disputes of jealousy, bad manners, and mindless pranks as if they had always been together and treated both parent and stepparent with apparent respect and affection. America bought it, romanticizing the uniqueness of that family. Today, there is nothing unique about combined families, the numbers having risen dramatically in the last 45 years (Gosselin & David, 2007; Jones, 2003; Lewis & Kreider, 2015). The rise in combined families has opened our collective eyes to just how fictitious the television stepfamily depictions of *The Brady Bunch* (and later *Eight is Enough*; Moore, 1977–1981) truly were (Carter & McGoldrick, 2005a; Jones, 2003). While the growing numbers of stepfamilies have reduced their uniqueness as a family unit, growing interest in these families as worthy of scholarly and clinical study has uncovered the distinctiveness within each stepfamily.

The dynamics of each stepfamily is shaped by the personalities involved and the dynamics of previous relationships. The diverse composition of stepfamilies (biological parent, stepparent, child, stepchild, mutual child plus one, or perhaps two ex-spouses plus extended present and ex-family members) generates multiple levels of initial tension around the simultaneous adjustment to new and multiple roles and relationships. Conflicts are rooted in insecurity, brought on by the uncertainty of how to enact these roles while living them at the same time. Similar dynamics apply to those grown children whose parents remarry (Harris, 2014). Children coming into a combined family are most often those who have experienced either a divorce between their natural parents or the death of a parent. Their emotional senses have been brought to new heights. The foundation they once held as stable and solid is gone, and life is no longer routine (Jones, 2003). Stepparents often find themselves the brunt of these frustrations and fears. This is uncharted water for everyone; "our culture lacks any established patterns or rituals to help handle the complex relationships of acquired family members" (Carter & McGoldrick, 2005b, p. 417; Gold, 2009).

In addition to the stepparent–stepchild relationship, clinicians must remember to attend to the marital relationship, which tends to be overshadowed by the stepparent roles (Halford, Nicholson, & Sanders, 2007) and to the effects of having "my," "your," and perhaps "our" children all sharing the same home. Yet one more issue revolves around how ex-spouses can collaborate as effective coparents, resolving whatever acrimony remains from the marriage for the sake of long-term shared child rearing (Mahoney, 2006). What must become clear to clinicians is that the old myths of the stepfamily drastically interfere with effective clinical understanding and therapeutic assistance to these family constellations. Therefore, clinicians must educate themselves beyond comparisons with nuclear families to truly appreciate the unique strengths and challenges in working with a family system whose numbers are predicted to become the dominant family form in the United States in the 21st century (Jones, 2003).

Because the numbers of stepfamilies are increasing, their rate of failure is a matter of concern. In the United States, the divorce rate for first marriages for both parties hovers at about 50%. That figure includes both formal divorces and those permanent separations that do not result in divorce (Stanley, 2015). More than 60% of second marriages fail. Stepfamily formation is not culture-bound but appears throughout all cultures, signifying the diversity of this family form and its identified struggles. Success in a stepfamily is more difficult than in a nuclear family; all the more reason for directed research and practical publications to assist clinicians to honor the unique dynamics in stepfamilies and to have a resource to guide thoughtful, practical, and empirically validated interventions (Jones, 2003).

This final thought forms the purpose of this work. Clinicians in training and those in practice need to understand the evolution of stepfamilies; use a developmental schema to pinpoint and legitimize normative transition issues and to diagnose those issues that exceed normative patterns; distinguish marital and stepparenting issues; grasp the similar and differing issues facing stepfather, stepmother, and mutual-child stepfamilies; learn short-term interventions supported with empirical validation to intervene effectively with both subsystems; and understand how to integrate extended family members' needs, such as those of ex-spouses and grandparents, into clinical service and how to prepare the stepfamily to appreciate its unique growth and yet common challenges.

Current Resources for Counseling Stepfamilies

This review and analysis of available assets was conducted in 2013 and updated in Spring 2015. The available publications tended to fall into two categories: clinician-focused works (very few) and self-help books (many).

The search for existing training books revealed two 2011 publications. One book presented a psychological model focusing on this topic, advocating dividing the stepfamily in order to treat each member separately. The book offered typical diagnostic classifications of differing stepfamily members with suggestions for treatment. This orientation seems congruent with the authors' professional orientations as psychologists but inconsistent with the family or systemic focus that is offered in this book. The second book offered a description of stepfamilies based on sociological precepts, but it could not provide family counselors with strategies or interventions suitable for this population.

The wealth of self-help books that were evaluated consistently offered behavioral interventions for families and couples but scant direction for clinicians as to how to understand and facilitate interpersonal problem solving. The popularity of these self-help books clearly confirms that they fill a need. However, the self-help genre seems to overlook family member insight as a precursor to family behavioral change, a position that I adopt in this book.

A Family Systems Clinical Approach

This book and the interventions proposed in the various chapters are grounded in the principles of family systems and in the notion that issues, and their resolution, arise between individuals rather than within one person. This distinction implies that the focus of attention, therefore, cannot be simply on an individual (e.g., the "stepdad" or the "stepchild") but rather on the interaction of the entire stepfamily on a single confounding issue, such as discipline or conflict resolution. This statement suggests that the self-help approach, though attractive, is unlikely to be helpful because it is based on the assumption that the key issue rests in the enactment of mutually agreed-upon roles and functions.

For example, if a father and son are in conflict about an issue, there is no doubt or ambiguity surrounding the parent–child relationship. Father has been a parent, in some fashion, since the son's birth and holds all the rights and responsibilities of a parent. The son, likewise, has experienced only this father and has been reared within the "son" role specific to this family. Moreover, those role definitions and enactments reflect socially acceptable expressions of being a father and a son, with referents in social institutions such as extended family, church, and so on.

In the case of a stepfather and stepson, however, none of these certainties exist. There is no history of relationship or experience being "fathered" by this adult; and, in fact, the fathering was probably provided by another male figure, the biological father. The question can be raised as to what role definition and enactment coincides with the creation of the stepfamily. Further, the child may still have contact with the biological father and has a preexisting notion of "son" with that adult. This conundrum could be simply resolved by adherence to social dictates on how to fulfill the stepfather and stepson roles. However, no such social mores around stepfamily roles exist. Instead of the certainty of widespread established relational descriptions and enactments, as pertains to nuclear family roles, there exists ongoing ambiguity and confusion as to how to make the best of the stepfamily situation. The lack of institutionalization of the stepfamily roles is an issue that I explore in this book.

Given the absence of guidance, social "myths" describing the differing stepfamily roles fill the vacuum of social guidelines. Assuming that each stepfamily member "creates" his or her own "stepfamily myths" about interacting with the various persons within that family unit, attention to those myths, as a way to explain the conflict-ridden behavioral patterns, must precede any attempts to change the pattern themselves. This exercise then allows each person to learn the discrepant myths that characterize the interaction styles of each family member. In addition, the creation of conjoint stepfamily myths allows each member to contribute to this "script" for how to be a stepfamily.

Narrative Therapy: Rationale and Possibility

Narrative therapy is the clinical lens for this entire book and the suggested interventions contained in each chapter. In this section, I provide a brief six-step synopsis of this model; interested readers should refer to Morgan (2000) and Phipps and Vorster (2015).

1. *Identify Dominant Social Narratives*
   A key assumption of narrative therapy is that knowledge is constructed rather than discovered (Nichols, 2011), and any event can embody multiple meanings and interpretations. Santos, Goncalves, and Matos (2011) suggested that clients "mis-identify with socially-constructed and maintained stories that are proving problematical in their lives" (p. 131). According to Goldenberg and Goldenberg (2013), our problems are maintained through stories we tell about ourselves and the world we inhabit, which explain our current actions and affect our future. These narratives tend to be negative, self-defeating myths, so that what we notice fits into a preestablished story. If the meaning and perception are changed, then new action will follow. Williams and Kurtz (2009) described "story-telling as a way to transmit family and cultural values that guide personal expectations and actions" (p. 174). They cautioned about the "impact of cultural experience on the members of diverse groups who remain outside the dominant cultural narratives of any culture" (p. 175), such as stepfamilies, whose structure and functioning are seen as poor in comparison to that of the nuclear family.
2. *Deconstruct the Dominant Social Narratives*
   "Problems arise as people subscribe to narrow and self-defeating views of themselves and the world" (Williams & Kurtz, 2009, p. 176). Nichols (2011) claimed that people struggle against a problem and that they can separate from the problem by identifying unique outcomes

or experiences when the problem is resisted or they act in ways that contradict the problem story. Williams and Kurtz (2009) argued that any situation or relationship holds endless possibilities for alternative meanings, which lead to alternative ways of acting, as individuals behave in response to selected information, meaning, and significance. This recognition of exception or unique outcomes dismantles the "thin" descriptions imposed from dominant social narratives, which lead to disempowering descriptions and obscures the positive characteristics of the relationship (Goldenberg & Goldenberg, 2013).

3. *Reauthor the Narratives That Guide Stepfamily Functioning*

   The key aspect of reauthoring dominant narratives seems founded less in radical revision than in discovery of what is lived daily. Additionally, narrative therapists believe that clients have the competencies to construct positive stories. Alternative plots seek to contrast differing lights on similar situations, implying that the challenge and emotional pain rests not in the event or the other person but rather in the perception made of that event (Goldenberg & Goldenberg, 2013). The resource for these new narratives is found within family interactions themselves (Santos et al., 2011) by bringing to light and magnifying trivialized unique outcomes. These outcomes, too often ignored, offer a template for a preferred style of meaning making and interaction. As exceptions to the dominant narrative, these alternative outcomes seem deviant, while, all along, it is their very message that contains the seeds of change. Nichols (2011) suggested anchoring these new perspectives by asking clients to focus on more optimistic accounts of experience through effects questions (e.g., How does this new view affect you? Your attitudes? Your ideas about yourself? Your relationships?).

4. *Turn Narrative Into Action*

   According to Santos et al. (2011), new experiences are based on the removal of the constraints of dominant narrative, allowing clients to envision and reflect on alternative ways of acting. The emphasis on unique outcomes and their "thickening" (Goldenberg & Goldenberg, 2013) entails their emphasis over the problem-focused dominant narratives and provides clients with personally created and implemented relational styles. (Here, *thickening* denotes the more positive narratives or stories that clients create to offset the dominant social narratives that portray negative experiences.) Therefore, the focus is greater on "remembering" rather than "remediating." Reinforcement of these more positive experiences can be found in the reflection-on-action moments advocated by Santos et al. (2011), in which the focus of evaluation turns from the "other" to the "self" and is related to enactment of the new self-constructed narratives. Nichols (2011) described the importance of finding audiences to support one's progress and to confirm one's change.

5. *Evaluate Positive Change and Growth*

   Clients now have two narratives for any situation: the original problem-focused dominant narrative and the newly created unique outcome-based narrative. Given the relative novelty of the second narrative, diligence is required to firmly anchor that fledgling perspective and remain positive in one's orientation. Clients can be asked to identify mechanisms that prevent change and markers of stability (Santos et al., 2011). These markers of sabotage are not meant to legitimize non-change but to provide an anticipatory point of reference for which the client can plan resistance. Markers of stability demonstrate positive change and foster perseverance and applied effort.

6. *Anticipate Setbacks and Future Challenges*
   Williams and Kurtz (2009) warned clients to recognize the pervasiveness of problem-oriented narratives. These generalities may interfere with clients' best-intentioned actions. However, anticipation of setbacks is part of normalizing this process of experimentation and success, and clients are to be congratulated on their recognition. The greater the emotionality of the situation, the greater the potential for setbacks, urging clients to "emote" after the interaction, rather than during or before, and to honor the challenge of personal direction and change in the face of an obdurate and persistent widespread message of how to be a stepfamily and stepfamily members.

In summary, narrative therapists share four common assumptions about people (Nichols, 2011):

1. People have good intentions.
2. They are profoundly influenced by external discourses.
3. When they distance themselves from their problems, they are able to develop empowering stories.
4. They are capable of de-internalizing dominant cultural myths.

Narrative therapy has been used in empirically validated studies on a range of topics, including attention to relationship therapy, mental illness, anorexia/bulimia, gay and lesbian issues, and substance abuse (Williams & Kurtz, 2009). However, attention to stepfamily functioning has yet to be documented (Jones, 2003), an omission I hope to correct through this book.

Issues of Diversity

Any significant contribution to the professional literature on stepfamilies in the 21st century, and beyond, must consider the effect of cultural diversity on these families. This theme is included in all the training, ethical codes, and accreditation standards that govern the professions of likely readers of this book. The central question, then, is which issues of diversity are relevant. I reviewed the glossary of the most recent standards adopted by the Council for Accreditation of Counseling and Related Educational Programs (2015) and found the following 11 terms under the heading of *multiculturalism*: racial heritage, ethnic heritage, cultural heritage, socioeconomic status, age, gender, sexual orientation, religious/spiritual beliefs, physical abilities, emotional abilities, and mental abilities.

To determine which of these categories is relevant to the understanding of stepfamily dynamics, I conducted a literature search and cross-referenced each term with *stepfamily* to secure the broadest response; I found scholarly work focusing on African American stepfamilies, Latino stepfamilies, gay stepfamilies, and lesbian stepfamilies. Therefore, I will refer to these four groups to discuss diversity in stepfamily dynamics.

Roadmap and Audience

This book on stepfamilies and stepfamily membership is organized in the following manner. It begins with an introduction to stepfamily demographics and what is known and believed about them as families (Chapter 1), followed by a presentation of developmental schemas of stepfamilies (Chapter 2). Attention then turns to marital issues (Chapter 3) and step-parenting issues (Chapter 4) before focusing on specific types of stepfamily constellations: stepfather stepfamilies (Chapter 5), stepmother stepfamilies (Chapter 6), and mutual-child stepfamilies (Chapter 7). The extended stepfamily constellation members (ex-spouses) are discussed in Chapter 8; grandparents/stepgrandparents are the focus of Chapter 9. The concluding chapter offers directions for future professional development. I approach this topic from a narrative therapy orientation, assuming that recognizing dominant scripts around stepfamily roles and functioning must precede reauthorship of those family ideals, leading logically to interventions designed to promote behavioral change (Jones, 2003). I supplement the text with first-person accounts from stepfamily members that were posted on stepfamily-oriented sites. Each chapter ends with a list of resources for both clinicians and family members that are readily available on the Internet.

The intended target audience includes all counselors and mental health professionals seeking to provide understanding, legitimization, and facilitation of stepfamily development. A review of professional training standards across disciplines such as counseling, social work, psychology, and marriage and family therapy indicates a need for sensitivity to diverse family issues. This book is intended to focus on stepfamily dynamics through the lens of systems thinking and narrative therapy, with the concomitant assumption that readers of this book have sufficient foundational knowledge in both topics. If not, readers are strongly urged to acquire such seminal knowledge in order to make full and proper use of the information in this book. I also believe that, given its practical orientation, the book would be a welcome addition to the professional libraries of practicing clinicians. For those who have completed graduate degrees and licensure and seek guidance in how to conceptualize and intervene with stepfamilies, this book will serve those missions well.

Conclusion

Mental health clinicians will work with members of stepfamilies during their careers. Working with this family constellation places unique demands on clinicians; it is incumbent on them to concisely define those values and competencies that will foster successful stepfamilies and offset the high dissolution rates of second and subsequent marriages. "These are values that honor and respect kinship ties based on affection and moral responsibility, rather than biology alone" (Jones, 2003, p. 235) and, by so espousing these values and enactments of these values in each stepfamily, improve the stepfamily experience for all concerned.

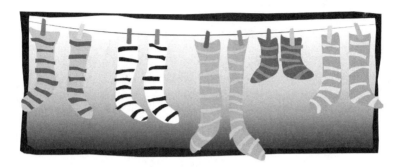

About the Author

Joshua M. Gold, PhD, is a professor in the Counselor Education Program
at the University of South Carolina. He completed his doctoral study at
Kent State University in 1991 and then served on the faculty of Fairfield
University for four years before joining the faculty at the University of
South Carolina in 1995. He is a member of International Association
of Marriage and Family Counselors and a contributing editorial board
member of *The Family Journal*. This book marks a reflective milepost
for him in a career that began in clinical work with stepfamilies, which
was the focus of his dissertation research and then remained a research
thread during his tenure as a professor.

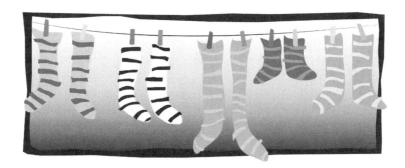

Acknowledgments

A scholarly work is improved by integrating the thoughtful feedback provided by expert reviewers. I gratefully acknowledge all who served as reviewers for different parts of this book. I also honor the support and guidance provided by Carolyn Baker, Nancy Driver, and the professionals at the American Counseling Association who helped me hone the thesis of this book. Their patience and input were critical to its evolution as I worked to strengthen the content while allowing my voice as an author to emerge.

My faculty colleagues in the Counselor Education program at the University of South Carolina have always encouraged my efforts as a professor; their steadfast support means a lot to me. Several graduate students in the educational specialist and doctoral degree programs at the university were interested in the topic of stepfamilies; they played a role in encouraging me to write this book.

This book reflects a blending of professional and lived experiences. When I began my clinical work almost 30 years ago, I was introduced to the complexities of stepfamily life and marveled at the commitment, dedication, and heartbreak that characterized stepfamily life. Those therapeutic successes and frustrations fueled my decision to focus on stepfamilies for my doctoral research, which I completed almost 25 years ago at Kent State University; I am grateful that my doctoral committee honored my interest. I have continued with the research theme over my career as a faculty member and expanded its relevance over the past decade in my role and experiences as a remarried spouse to Hope, a stepfather to Aia and Della, and father of Will, my child with Hope. It has been fascinating to me to integrate my professional knowledge and lived experience in the creation and evolution of this book.

This book has truly been a team effort. While my name will appear as author, I could not have written it without the contributions of the individuals mentioned above.

Chapter 1

Introduction:
What We Know About Stepfamilies

Stepfamily constellations represent a growing societal trend (Lewis & Kreider, 2015; McGoldrick & Carter, 2011), and clinicians are almost guaranteed to work with stepfamily dynamics during the course of their careers. This book will draw on what is known about African American, Latino, gay, and lesbian stepfamilies in order to explore issues of cultural diversity within this specific context.

Two terms are used to describe the family constellation and its attendant dynamics that are the focus of this book. To my mind, *stepfamily* refers to a family system in which one of the spouses has previous children, and *blended family* denotes families in which both spouses have children from prior unions. In both instance, the number of external prior and evolving relationships remain the same. Within the family unit, the term *stepchild* is used to distinguish the child to whom one spouse is not the biological parent, while the generic term *child* refers to a spouse's biological offspring.

This chapter will provide demographic data on stepfamilies in the United States, followed by a description of common social myths about stepfamilies and comments from stepfamily members about their lives. Each dominant social myth is deconstructed to illustrate that application of narrative therapy to these popular notions regarding stepfamily life. Subsequent chapters explore myths about specific roles within the stepfamily system.

Stepfamily Demographic Data

A *stepfamily* is defined as a household in which two adults are in a committed couple relationship and where at least one of the adults has a child or

1

children from a previous relationship. Those children may be in residence, be jointly parented, or have reached an age of majority and left the family home. An estimated 9,100 new American stepfamilies are created each week. Fifty percent of all Americans have a step connection (Stewart, 2007). It is predicted that the stepfamily constellation will be the most common family form in the United States by 2020 (Visher & Visher, 2003).

The actual demographic data on stepfamilies seems more difficult to discern. Standard reporting systems, such as the U.S. Census, tend to underestimate the numbers of stepfamilies, because of either the lack of an agreed upon definition of what actually constitutes a stepfamily or budgetary constraints, resulting in the absence of marriage, divorce, and stepfamily reporting. Data collection may be confounded by living arrangements that do not include formal marriage and multi-household families in which children move between two or more households (Crosbie-Burnett et al., 2005; Deal, 2014; Lewis & Kreider, 2015; Pew Research Center, 2011). Data collection that allows for such variation will provide researchers and clinicians with more accurate numbers of stepfamilies.

The emergence of stepfamilies in ever-growing numbers challenges family counselors to replace the "nuclear family" norm with more current exemplars of family dynamics relevant to, and stemming from, the stepfamily experience (Felker, Fromme, Arnaut, & Stoll, 2002; Goldenberg & Goldenberg, 2002; Gosselin & David, 2007). Stepfamilies have always formed part of the family constellation of society; however, the recent growth of divorce rates and subsequent remarriages have expanded their numbers (Goldenberg & Goldenberg, 2002; Inhinger-Tallman & Cooney, 2005). Four recent U.S. presidents (Barack Obama, Bill Clinton, Ronald Reagan, and Gerald Ford) were members of stepfamilies.

An initial examination of the data describing the context of family diversity will serve to substantiate the numbers and growth of stepfamilies in America. Carter and McGoldrick (2005b) claimed that "more than ½ of Americans today have been, are now or will eventually be in one or more stepfamilies during their lives" (p. 417). According to Pew Research Center (2011) data and Lewis and Kreider (2015), more than 40% of adults have at least one steprelative in their family. While initially stepfamilies were formed when widows or widowers remarried, more recently divorced adults are remarrying and forming stepfamilies. In 2002, 55% of first marriages ended in divorce (Gately, Pike, & Murphy, 2006); more recent data lower that figure to about 50% if both legal divorces and long-term separations are combined (Stanley, 2015), and a majority of those adults (65% of women and 70% of men) will remarry (Portrie & Hill, 2005; Wilkes & Fromme, 2002). Usually women remarry within 3–5 years and men remarry within 1–2 years of the dissolution of the previous relationship (Gately et al., 2006), and either one or both partners most often bring children to the new union (Mahoney, 2006). The result is that 33% of all Americans are in stepfamily relationships (Malia, 2005), including an estimated 10 million stepchildren under the age of 18 (Wilkes & Fromme, 2002).

2

Some demographic statistics are relevant to understanding the stepfamily numbers. Unless otherwise noted, the data are from the U.S. Census Bureau (2007), the most recent data available.

- About 35 million Americans in the U.S. are remarried.
- An additional 36 million Americans are divorced or widowed (possibly finding themselves in a remarriage at some point).
- About 46% of all marriages today are a remarriage for one or both partners, and about 65% of remarriages involve children from the prior marriage and, thus, form stepfamilies.
- Approximately one third of all weddings in America today form stepfamilies (Deal, 2014).
- The divorce rate for remarried and stepfamily couples varies but is at least 60% (Falke & Larson, 2007).
- Second marriages (with or without children) have a 60% rate of divorce, and 73% of third marriages end in divorce (U.S. Census Bureau, 2006); at least two thirds of stepfamily couples divorce and divorce occurs more quickly in stepfamilies than first marriages (Halford et al., 2007; Michaels, 2006)
- An estimated one third of children will live in a stepparent home before the age of 18 (Parker, 2007), and 50% will have a stepparent at some point in their lifetime (Deal, 2014; Stewart, 2007).
- An estimated 40% of women will live in a married or cohabiting stepfamily home at some point (Stewart, 2007).

These facts reveal the growing prevalence of stepfamilies in society as a whole (Lewis & Kreider, 2015).

Issues of Cultural Diversity and Stepfamily Demographics

As stated in the Preface, this book will discuss four culturally distinct groups of stepfamilies for which there is some research: Latino, African American, gay, and lesbian stepfamilies. (In this section only, gay and lesbian stepfamilies' demographic data are reported together.) All of these groups are underestimated and underreported in the literature (Pew Research Center, 2011).

Latinos currently made up 12.5% of the total U.S. population, and that percentage will grow to 24.4% by 2050 (Reck, Bigginbotham, Skogrand, & Davis, 2012). It has been reported that 16% of Latino children are members of stepfamilies (Inhinger-Tallman & Cooney, 2005). Plunkett, Williams, Schock, and Sands (2007) identified Latino stepfamilies as the fastest growing family structure within the Latino population (p. 5). In addition, 38% of women between the ages of 18 and 36 gave birth while they were unmarried, and they tend to view the current family system as a first marriage rather than as a stepfamily because there was no marriage to the father of the child/ren. In addition, divorce rates among Latinos mirror those rates of Caucasians, with a 52% divorce rate; 44% remarry within 4 years. In this population, repartnering seems more prevalent than does remarriage, removing these repartnered stepfamilies from any current categories used by formal census data collecting agencies.

Stewart (2007) decried "the few studies on racial and ethnic diversity" (p. 20), and Carey (2009) claimed that "an exhaustive review revealed an absence of the African American family in stepfamily research" (p. 2); a 2015 search of the literature suggests that nothing has been published in this area since Carey's 2009 review. Among African American families, confusion regarding the number of stepfamilies is based on the incidences of nonmarital births and the number of cohabiting couples. Cutrona, Russell, Burzette, Wesner, and Bryant (2011) determined that 54% of cohabiting couples had residential children. However, cohabiting arrangements or common-law marriages are not counted as family units. Adler-Baeder, Russell, et al. (2010) found that, in 2006, 70.7% of children born to African American mothers were nonmarital births, so marriage would actually be a first marriage rather than remarriage. This practice then further confounds accurate definitions of stepfamilies among this group and raises questions about the accuracy of data collection.

Gay and lesbian stepfamilies are "virtually ignored in stepfamily research" (Lynch, 2000, p. 82) and are "absent from most estimates of stepfamilies" (Stewart, 2007, p. 20). However, as Fredriksen-Goldsen and Erera (2003) noted, "significant numbers of gay and lesbian families have claimed the rights to raise children and live as a family" (p. 172). Lacking "hard" data, Crosbie-Burnett et al. (2005) estimated that gay and lesbian families account for 30% of households in the United States with children under 18, numbering between 2 and 8 million, and that gay and lesbian couples are raising 3–14 million children, a number which may increase based on the dissolution rates of gay and lesbian relationships and on the greater numbers of gay and lesbian individuals having children. Claxton-Oldfield and O'Neil (2007) reported that 22% of households headed by lesbians had residential children, compared to 5% of gay couples. Stewart (2007) estimated that 1 out of 9 cohabiting couples is same-sex; in the 2000 U.S. Census Bureau data, 33% of female same-sex households and 22% of male same-sex households include children. It is not known whether families where the child/ren predate the current relationship or whether the child/ren are a product of the current relationship would be categorized as a "stepfamily."

The number of stepfamilies is expected to exceed the number of nuclear families in the United States in the near future (Felker et al., 2002). The U.S. Census Bureau figures published in 2000 are said to have underestimated the actual number of stepchildren; only one "householder" is identified for census purposes, and the children could be those of the spouse but are not counted, as those children may not be the biological children of the identified head of household. Therefore, while official censuses cannot enumerate accurately the numbers of stepfamilies either in total or by specified culturally diverse groups, their numbers cannot be ignored (Michaels, 2006). Consequently, it is critical for family-focused mental health professionals to separate dominant social myths from reality where stepfamilies are concerned.

Myths About Stepfamilies

Portrayals of stepfamilies in popular television shows such as the *Brady Bunch* and *Eight is Enough* of stepmothers in fairy tales such as Cinderella, Snow White, Hansel and Gretel, and of either overly strict or abusive stepfathers influence both the family members and mental health professionals into distinctly biased views of stepfamilies (Jones, 2003). A basis for building a strong stepfamily is an understanding of its realities as well as a debunking of its myths and honoring its strengths. Understanding the myths and realities helps stepfamily members, and mental health professionals, appreciate what is normal as a stepfamily develops, leading to more reasonable expectations for family life.

Five of the most common myths about stepfamilies are described in the sections that follow (Jones, 2003).

Myth #1: Stepfamily Blending Happens Quickly

There is a conception that the proximity of two previously unconnected family systems will manifest itself into instantaneous affection and become an instant family, much like those affections portrayed on popular television, with the concurrent belief that the absence of such a transformation indicates pending failure for the new stepfamily. Given the incomplete institutionalization of stepfamily blending (Cherlin, 1978), caricatures found in popular media often suffice as actual exemplars. This dominant narrative also implies that the transition ought to be easily accomplished, with no relational setbacks along the way; disagreement on how to be a "stepfamily" or conflict as roles are negotiated and settled implies a weakness in the system or the poor selection of a partner/new stepparent. The expectations that transition should be seamless sets couples up with unreasonable expectations.

Myth #2: A Stepfamily Is the Same as a First Marriage Family

An uninformed observer might believe that all families with two adults and one or more children are comparable and that the current marriage must represent the initial marriage for each partner, obviating postdivorce or marital dissolution tensions, relations with ex-spouses, or the complexity of coparenting. This belief is based on several assumptions: that the marital relationship is the priority, that parents have equal authority, that the marital relationship has had time to solidify prior to the arrival of children, that the parents share an equal history with each child, and that no other affective ties exist between children and other parental figures. These assumptions vastly overlook the complexity of stepfamily dynamics.

Myth #3: Children Whose Parents Divorce and Remarry Are Damaged Permanently

There can be no disputing the pain and anger caused by marital divorce, custody proceedings, and the upheaval of every aspect of one's life for children of any age. Moreover, this upheaval is repeated with the introduction of a stepparent and perhaps stepsiblings. It is no wonder that loyalty conflicts and the uncertainty of stepfamily life take an emotional toll on children. This emotional toll may be expressed in inappropriate school behaviors, home conflicts, and social acting out. These easily recognizable "cries of distress" mislead others into thinking that the disruptiveness and trauma of this transition are normative and enduring. Moreover, it is easier to document those children struggling with this transition rather than those for whom the conversion to the stepfamily was an easier process.

Myth #4: Children Need to Withdraw From Their Nonresidential Parent to Bond With a Stepparent

Consistent with the legal perspective that a child can have only two parents, children are sometimes expected to relinquish any expectation of the divorced parent as active and involved and, equally traumatically, to replace that spouse with an individual with whom the child shares no family history and a negligible emotional connection. The myth is premised on the belief that continued contact and emotional attachment with the nonresidential parent will interfere with the transition to the new stepfamily. Just as one's parent has "replaced" the divorced spouse with the new spouse, so too are children to "divorce" the parent who no longer resides in the family home and instead to replace that parent figure with the new stepparent.

Myth #5: Remarriages That Follow a Death Go More Smoothly Than Those That Occur After a Divorce

There is an assumption that the physical passing of a spouse/parent equates to an emotional relinquishment of that relationship and that stepfamilies that form after a death will evolve easily because the new stepparent can fill the relational void. This belief is influenced in part by comparing the stepfamily formed when divorced adults remarry; the divorced spouse remains a "present" parent, confounding the status of the new stepparent and generating loyalty conflicts between the children and the new parental holon.

Narratives: Stepfamily Members Describe Their Own Lives

The following comments are examples of the countless postings on Internet chat rooms.

> Everyone has a compelling story to tell. Every single person within a stepfamily structure could break your heart with their side of things. I try to remember that in my own stepfamily life when I want to lash out because I'm hurt or angry or just grieving that I'm in a stepfamily at all at the same time that I'm happy I'm in one. It's complicated. Our families are all complicated. But it's so easy to get stuck in our own version of things. When I read angry, hurtful letters and comments on this site I see deep pain.
> —Retrieved from http://www.noonesthebitch.com (10/29/2012)

To survive and have a successful marriage is no easy task. Stir in children from a previous marriage, ex-spouses, ex-in-laws, and the extra baggage from previous relationships and you will realize just how different the stepfamily is. Each of these ingredients can bring with it a whole set of problems themselves that need to be dealt with.

—Retrieved from http://www.hicow.com/stepfamily/marriage/
invisible-man-1.html (10/29/2012)

As a step and bio Mom, I know that it is not uncommon for tension, compromise, and confusion to rule when the role of parent is shared between a step and biological parent. Some people still feel that stepparents aren't "real" parents, but our culture has no norms to suggest how they are different. And the less our roles are defined, the more unhappy we are as both parents and stepparents. Another role ambiguity is that society seems to expect acquired parents and children to instantly love each other in much the same way as biological parents and their children do. In reality, however, this is often just not so. A stepparent might feel a tremendous amount of guilt about his or her lack of positive feelings (or even the presence of negative feelings) toward the spouse's children. As a stepparent, you might feel like an unbiased observer with a grudge because you're an outsider and the very thing that's making you "unbiased" is something you resent, biology. Stepchildren, as well, often don't react to their parent's new spouse as though he or she were the "real" parent. The irony of expecting instant "real" parent-child love is further complicated by the fact that stepparents are not generally expected to be "equal" in discipline or otherwise controlling their stepchildren. Another reason for a difficult stepparent-child relationship might be that your child does not want this marriage to work, and so, acts out with hostility. Commonly children harbor fantasies that their biological parents will reunite. If children had reservations about or strongly disapproved of your divorce, they may sabotage your new relationships in the hope that you will get back together. Children who want their natural parents to remarry may feel that sabotaging the new relationship will get them back together. Although all stepchildren and stepparents are to some degree uncomfortable with some aspect of their new family role, certain difficulties are more likely to affect stepmothers, and others are more common to stepfathers. As a stepparent, your best shot at happiness is to ignore the myths and negative images and to work to stay optimistic. Society also seems, on the one hand, to expect romantic, almost mythical loving relationships between stepmothers and children while, at the same time, portraying stepmothers as cruel, vain, selfish, competitive, and even abusive.

—Retrieved from http://becomingastepmom.wordpress.com (10/29/2012)

Deconstructing the Myths

Narrative-theory clinicians believe that clients commonly "report a sense of helplessness and blame-filled descriptions of each member and the relationships between them" (Williams & Kurtz, 2009, p. 182). It is the adherences to these problem-saturated descriptions, not the individuals involved, which constitute the focus of deconstruction. The process of deconstruction provides a critical analysis of texts to establish that the dominant narratives are simply that; one possible story or explanation for an event. When clients accept this, generating alternative explanations, founded in the client's lived experience and clinician's professional knowledge, becomes possible (Goldenberg & Goldenberg, 2013; Nichols, 2011; Williams & Kurtz, 2009). Out of those thickened narratives, which replace the dominant social narratives, come new ways to foster a more realistic and empowering vision of shared stepfamily values and beliefs.

Deconstructing Myth #1: Stepfamily Blending Happens Quickly

It can take anywhere from 4 to 7 years for a stepfamily to blend successfully (Visher & Visher, 1996, 2003; Visher, Visher, & Pasley, 1997). One rule of thumb is that, for each child, the evolution process takes twice as long as the child's chronological age at the time of the stepfamily formation. Therefore, the process of stepfamily bonding, assuming all other dynamics are equal, will happen more quickly for younger children and more slowly the older the child; in fact, family bonding may never occur if the stepchildren are teens. As discussed in the next chapter, this process involves five distinct developmental stages, each of which must be completed successfully to meet the challenges of later stages.

When stepfamily members buy into the myth of "instant blending," they may think that something is wrong with their family when it seems to take a long time for things to settle down. This may turn into self-blaming, leading one partner (usually the stepparent) to withdraw from the new family system. Questioning the system itself or one's place within that system bodes poorly for its continuity. This dismay may be part of the reason for the greater rate of dissolution of second, and subsequent, marriages (about 65%) during the first 3 years. If one believes that the turmoil and stress of transition are permanent features of the relationship, stepparents may be tempted to give up on their new family prematurely.

Deconstructing Myth #2:
A Stepfamily Is the Same as a First-Marriage Family

Stepfamily members may have a tendency to inappropriately compare their family to the "ideal" first-marriage families they know. The professional literature labels this tendency as a "deficiency comparison model" (Carter & McGoldrick, 2005a). In theory, a "deficit comparison" approach is based on appraisals between one normative experience and deviant experiences, with those experiences that do not match the normative model decried as inferior. However, the very real differences between stepfamilies and first-marriage families should be seen not as deficiencies in the stepfamily but rather as expressions of its uniqueness. Stepfamily development is more complex and challenging than nuclear family development (see Chapter 2), and part of the complexity derives from the lack of societal institutionalization for the roles and functioning in the stepfamily. (*Social institutionalization* refers to a set of common practices that seem to epitomize the way that different social groups tend to behave; Cherlin, 1978.) This notion can be compared to a floor plan for a home that allows for individual expression but adheres to commonly accepted practice in construction. This type of "family blueprint" does not yet exist for stepfamilies, which means that individuals often experience apprehension and wonder whether they are doing things "right."

Deconstructing Myth #3: Children Whose Parents Divorce and Remarry Are Damaged Permanently

The assertion of "permanent dysfunction" among children of divorce and in stepfamilies seems to generalize a point-in-time evaluation of a child's functioning without adequate reassessment over time. Clearly the initial period of stepfamily formation may be difficult, as individuals find that their roles and relationships are reconfigured with external family members, such as non-residential parents and grandparents. This instability may manifest itself in children's school and social behaviors. However, this "acting out" is a symptom of the uncertainty of the stepfamily and will resolve itself over time with appropriate intervention to help the child/ren understand the stepfamily evolution and how to navigate a more complex relational web; extreme expressions of uncertainty and anger generally wane over time as the stepfamily system settles itself.

Nevertheless, about a third of children of divorce have long-term adjustment difficulties, usually as a function of continued conflict between the ex-spouses, not as a function of inclusion in the stepfamily. In these instances, children are "emotional victims" of the anger, resentment, and loyalty conflicts between their parents; the stepfamily processes and integration itself is not a factor. When divorced parents can construct effective coparenting relationships, their children adjust and are satisfied in their new families.

Deconstructing Myth #4: Children Need to Withdraw From Their Nonresidential Parent to Bond With a Stepparent

Divorce or spousal separation speaks to the dissolution of marital ties but states nothing about the dissolution of parent–child relationships. In the best of circumstances, continued contact between children and the absent biological parent affirms for the child the continued love, affection, and support of the absent parent. When children aren't allowed contact with the nonresidential parent, they tend to have idealized fantasies about him or her. Left without occasional "reality checks," children may develop expectations to which a stepparent can never fully measure up. Normally, the best situation for a child's growth and development is continued contact with both biological parents after divorce. This suggestion flies in the face of legal statute, which firmly states that a child can only have two "parents." However, this legal stipulation overlooks the emotional needs and reality of children in stepfamilies. In recognition of those needs, it is suggested

9

that stepfamily imaging include how the biological parents and stepparents can all contribute to meeting the emotional needs of all children involved, in a way that calls on the strengths of each stepfamily adult member and forms an overt commitment to set aside any lingering spousal animosity for the sake of the children.

Deconstructing Myth #5: Remarriages That Follow a Death Go More Smoothly Than Those That Occur After a Divorce

It can be simply asserted that remarriage is a complex reorganization of family affective ties, regardless of how the prior relationship ended. While home may be more peaceful following an acrimonious divorce, children may view the remarriage as a betrayal of the absent parent, for whom the children retain strong ties of history and affection, regardless of the parent's choice of a new partner. The separation of the roles of "husband" and "father," one now passed and the other still active, remains a residue from the legal battles of the divorce, requiring present and absent spouses to resolve any lingering marital issues or, at least, to ensure that those issues do not contaminate ongoing coparenting. The issues also emerge in cases of a parent's death. A parent who has died may also acquire a "halo," or image of perfection that makes it very difficult for a stepparent to enter and integrate with the new family. The physical absence of the departed spouse cannot be confused with the children's relinquishment of emotional attachments, some of which may grow even stronger in the absence of the deceased spouse as selective memory paints an idealized version of that parent. In addition, any attempt to convince the children that the new parent will "replace" the deceased parent will end poorly. Rather, the approach should be to augment rather than replace a parental role. Legally, children can only have two parents at any given time, but in their hearts, children can hold room for multiple parenting figures, each providing love, acceptance, and nurturance in unique ways.

This section has offered five examples of the deconstruction of popular dominant narratives about stepfamilies. If there is truth and guiding principle in the statement that "knowledge is power," then this process of replacing what society thinks with what the clinician knows and the stepfamily lives on a daily basis provides a counterbalance to the prevalent myths. While this transition needs to be translated into new interaction styles, the replacement of myths that foster confusion and hopelessness with more realistic and positive perspectives is a critical foundation.

Conclusion

The number of stepfamilies in society as a whole and among specified culturally diverse populations is growing, and clinicians are likely to encounter them in their practices. Clinicians would do well to consider how best to make stepfamily relationships more satisfactory and perhaps to offset the rise in the dissolution rate of second and subsequent marriages. As McGoldrick and Carter (2011, p. 317) advised, "the key that determines whether the issue is transitional or has permanent crippling impact is whether it is handled adequately within the family system in spite of the general lack of social support offered by society." Therefore, family empowerment and advocacy, based on the integration of professional knowledge and lived experience, is a critical step toward understanding the distinction between what society purports and what the professional literature reveals about stepfamilies.

Resources

Anonymous. (2011). *A portrait of stepfamilies*. Pew Research Center. Retrieved from http://www.pewsocialtrends.org/2011/01/13/

A presentation and analysis of emerging demographic trends in stepfamilies

Duncan, S. F. (n.d.). *Recognizing stepfamily myths, realities, and strengths*. Forever Families. Retrieved from https://foreverfamilies.byu.edu/Pages/stepfamilies/Recognizing-Stepfamily-Myths,-Realities,-and-Strengths.aspx

A listing of seven stepfamily myths and strengths

Lintermans, G. (2011). *Replace stepfamily myths with realistic expectations*. Retrieved from http://stepfamilysolutions.blogspot.com/2011/07/replace-stepfamily-myths-with-realistic.html

A self-report to normalize the complexity of stepfamily relationships

Stewart, S. D. (2006). *Brave new stepfamilies*. National Healthy Marriage Resource Center. Retrieved from www.healthymarriageinfo.org/

A presentation and analysis of emerging demographic trends in stepfamilies

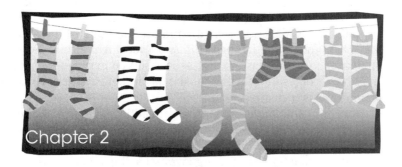

Chapter 2

Developmental Schemas
of Stepfamilies

In this chapter, I examine the social myths around stepfamily roles through the perspective of narrative theory. This therapeutic perspective represents a critical orientation to the concerns presented by stepfamily members within the counseling context (Portrie & Hill, 2005).

Counselors have three paradigms through which to approach stepfamily dynamics (Baxter, Braithwaite, & Nicholson, 1999; Stewart, 2007). One paradigm seeks to focus on stepfamily issues as unrelated episodes, in which differing family members play complementary roles (e.g., persecutor and victim). Issues include stepparenting, discipline, finances, living arrangements, relationships with nonresidential spouses, and the addition of a new child. By concentrating on the details of the latest conflict and the differing personalities involved, however, the clinician and family members are likely to lose sight of "the larger picture." A second paradigm seeks to isolate the "problem" or impediment to stepfamily success (e.g., the stepchild or stepparent) and labors through individual counseling to "cure" that one person. Such an approach is predicated on the tenets of individual counseling and is difficult to reconcile with a systemic orientation, which advocates focus on the relationships among individuals (Stewart, 2007). A third paradigm is a developmental orientation to understanding, intervening with, and facilitating the success of stepfamilies. However, "limited work has taken the developmental matters of the blended family on its own terms" (Baxter et al., 1999, p. 292). This chapter will briefly describe two differing developmental schemas and link the developmental orientation with the practice of narrative therapy.

A Developmental Orientation to Stepfamily Success

Family development theory provides an approach to studying families that is useful in explaining patterned change, the dynamic nature of the family, and how change occurs in the family life cycle. Originating in the 1930s as sociologists and demographers establish family categories (as precursors to family stages of development), and associated with the efforts of Paul Glick, Evelyn Duvall, Reuben Hill, and Rachel Ann Edwards, family development theory explains the processes observed in families over time. This progress becomes more critical as the incomplete institutionalization of stepfamily life is measured.

This concept of incomplete institutionalization is based on Cherlin's (1978) assertion of a "lack of social structures that organize, direct and execute the essential tasks of living" (Stewart, 2007, p. 39). These institutions (e.g., the legal system, faith-based organizations, the medical community) are really social authorities that define appropriate functioning between members in social relationships and between those family systems and the broader society. In the absence of frameworks for stepfamily relationships, socially held negative perceptions of stepfamilies form the basis of dominant social narratives. These narratives, which lack correspondence to the lived experience of members of stepfamilies, generate "negative labels, stereotypes and cultural myths" (Stewart, 2007, p. 41).

Stepfamilies evolve through processes of change and adjustment (McGoldrick & Carter, 2011, p. 317; see also Goldenberg & Goldenberg, 2002). Stepfamily life represents a complex interactive process whose goal is to forge a family identity and sense of cohesion among individuals with no common history, rituals, or behavior patterns. No wonder, then, that creation of a successful stepfamily has been identified as "one of the most difficult transitions a family is ever called upon to make" (Stewart, 2007, p. 182). Individual life cycle needs affect stepfamily task resolution—for example, an older male with adult children marrying a younger woman with young children, coping with loss of prior marriages or relationships, living with difference, resolving loyalty issues, acknowledging the absent parent, living simultaneously in two households, developing a family identity, overcoming boundary problems, learning coparenting, and involving a stepparent despite little social support. Individuals have to determine the tasks that must be done, the priority to give each one, and what guidance is available.

"Developmentalists focus on complexity and processes that occur within family systems as assess how these aspects of family life unfolds over time within a particular social context" (Stewart, 2007, p. 47). Rather than accept dominant and stereotypically negative descriptions of stepfamily members and stepfamily life, developmentalists observe how veritable strangers to one another form nourishing, reliable relationships; what challenges emerge in what sort of predictable order; and which resolutions seem critical for family identity and cohesion. A developmental map portrays what family experiments are normal and predictable within an overall picture of stepfamily evolution, as opposed to emphasizing family crisis (Stewart, 2007). Portrie and Hill (2005) proposed that such a "map" needs to be descriptive, to consider diversity, and to express dynamic shifts of blended family relationships, emphasizing the integration of individual and family developments, issues of solidarity and satisfaction as foundations to negotiate role identification, boundary management, and resolution of conflicts and expectations. The orderliness and predictability of this transition or evolution is part of the professional knowledge that the counselor may contribute to the session through educating all family members that their lived experience is in no way abnormal and their relationships in any way deficient. However, it is safe to say that very few stepfamily members are equipped with this knowledge, leaving them to concentrate on their frustrations with other family members or the latest stepfamily "crisis." By focusing on the issues facing remarriage and then stepfamily life, counselors focus attention on the present rather than issues in the past (e.g., relating to the family of origin). The intent is to provide guidance and reassurance as family members go through their days, to prevent overreaction to normative stepfamily experiences, and to foster the stepfamily maturation progression.

Family development theory divides the family experience into phases, or stages, over the life span and describes changes in family functioning and roles during each stage (Carter, McGoldrick, & Garcia-Preto, 2010). These changes imply distinctions in structure and role relationships within a given family unit. The stage is usually inferred from the events that indicate a change in the membership in the family or the way in which family members are spatially and interactionally organized (i.e., openly negotiated among family members). The successful completion of developmental tasks leads to immediate satisfaction and approval as well as to the increased potential for success with later tasks; failure results in family unhappiness, social disapproval, and greater difficulty with subsequent developmental tasks. For the family to continue to grow, biological requirements, cultural imperatives, and personal aspirations need to be satisfied during each stage of the family life cycle (Carter et al., 2010). To be successful, family members need to adapt to changing needs and demands of other family members and the changing expectations of the larger kin network and society. The stage theories specific to this topic do not provide, or impose, time frames and lengths; rather, task resolution determines transition to the next stage. Additionally, stage tasks are meant to be addressed completely and in a specific order. As with all stage theories, family development is undoubtedly a continuous process, but dividing the process into stages helps clinicians, and family members, see the tasks more clearly.

Stage Theories

Stewart (2007) described stage theories as a mixture of tools, concepts, hypotheses, and frameworks to explain stepfamily life. Lacking one grand theory as a function of the structural (race, class, gender), process (relationship quality, parenting style), and contextual (state laws, social attitudes)

15

variables characteristic of stepfamily life, these theories contradict the myth that stepfamilies cannot function as well as two-biological-parent families because of the absence of a biological connection to the children, thereby designating stepfamilies as inherently problematic. It can be safely asserted that stress in stepfamilies is different from that experienced in two-biological-parent families because of the diverse and conflicting notions of kinship, but this does not mean that stepfamily members are inherently poorer at dealing with stress than members of other family constellations—they simply need to be aware of how the stresses that they do face represent typical aspects of stepfamily life (McGoldrick & Carter, 2011).

Two complementary models of stepfamily development are described in this section. The first model, developed by Papernow (1999, as cited by www.steptogether.org), is divided into three stages, which are further subdivided; this overview is intended only to highlight specific stage tasks.

Early Stage

1. *Fantasy*:
   - Adults see the stepfamily as a healing crucible from the pain of divorce or bereavement.
   - Partners believe that since they love each other, stepparents and stepchildren will love each other too.
   - Stepparents dream of marrying nurturing parents, and single parents see stepparents as sharing parenting burden.
   - Children may fantasize about seeing parents back together or claiming an exclusive relationship with the biological parent.
2. *Immersion:*
   - All family members are immediately faced with the reality of the new family situation.
   - Stepparents encounter unexpectedly strong and negative feelings of jealousy, resentment, confusion, and inadequacy, because they are excluded by the spouse and children.
   - Biological parents may feel less uncomfortable because they have the support of the biological children.
   - The adults wonder about the lack of a spousal connection and the overemphasis on parenting or stepparenting.
   - Stepparents begin to internalize blame for all stepfamily conflict.
3. *Awareness:*
   - Stepfamily members begin putting names on painful feelings as a result of their family experiences.
   - A better understanding of the parent–biological child relationship allows for the observance of pattern and how those patterns may interfere with the strength of the spousal connection.
   - All members surrender fantasies of instant family.
   - The stepparent begins to get to know the strangers that he or she has joined.

The overarching challenge of the early stage is to bear the developmental tasks of confusion and disappointment without surrendering or dissolving the new stepfamily. As stepfamily members begin to articulate different experiences within the stepfamily and relinquish fantasies of the instant replication of the nuclear family, they can begin to engage in the step-by-step process of building a family out of strangers.

Middle Stage

4. *Mobilization:*
   - The couple openly airs differences.
   - This period tends to be chaotic and embattled.
   - The family members struggle between an "I" vs. "we" identity.
5. *Action:*
   - The adults jointly at first and then with the children negotiate new agreements about how the family will function.
   - The family structure changes, and new boundaries are drawn, especially between the couple and the children.
   - The family begins to function without constant monitoring of "step" issues.

Later Stage

6. *Contact:*
   - The family has arrived at the honeymoon period at last.
   - The moves of the "action" phase have provided new arenas of agreement within which the family members can function easily.
   - The marital relationship becomes more a source of nourishment and support.
   - Stepparents and children forge real relations, unhampered by "step" issues.
   - Only now can a clear stepparent role emerge.
7. *Resolution:*
   - The family is characterized by solid and reliable steprelations.
   - Norms are established, and a family-specific history is built that integrates prior family stories yet embraces the new.
   - Acceptance of differing levels of belonging on the part of different children is honored.
   - Large changes no longer threaten spousal or stepparent–stepchild relationship.

The key variable that determines whether one gets stuck or proceeds is the time it takes to negotiate the "awareness work" of the early stage: realizing that something is wrong, that it is not the fault of a single person, and that there is an opportunity to improve the situation and move on. Without this insight, family members would experience repeated and escalated conflicts, growing estrangement, and (as members become more hopeless) eventual stepfamily dissolution. Parents side with biological children against the stepparent and his/her children, further polarizing the stepfamily. In stepfamilies with only one stepparent, that adult feels ostracized within the stepfamily, drifting further and further from connection. The marital relationship, tenuous to begin with, dissolves under the pressure of parenting and stepparenting. The adults become so focused on the disagreements in parenting that being spouses becomes secondary in attention, and then tertiary as adults begin to focus on the "I," as an expression of emotional self-protection and identity, rather than the "we" of a couple.

Kerns (2009) offered a five-stage model for stepfamily development:

1. *Honeymoon/Fantasy:*
    -   The adults feel very positive about the new marriage and the integration of the stepparent and other children.
    -   However, the children have mixed feelings regarding the biological parent's new spouse and the imposition of "siblings."
    -   Each member holds different thoughts and expectations (e.g., parents hope for instant love, children secretly hope that their biological parents reconnect).
2. *Chaos:*
    -   The children feel disloyal to the absent biological parent if they like the stepparent.
    -   The parents feel constantly in the middle of stepparent and stepchild relations.
    -   The stepparents are excluded from old ways of running the household.
3. *Awareness:*
    -   The adults become aware that their problems are common.
    -   Change must occur, and it must start with each member (who may not be willing).
4. *Action:*
    -   Appropriate stepfamily issues are identified and addressed.
    -   Family members access support groups or family counseling.
    -   The adults unify to strengthen marital relationship.
    -   All family members try to understand how each other family member can see the same situation so differently.
5. *Commitment:*
    -   The adults, as models and then the children, move forward by collaborating and cooperating.
    -   The stepfamily members realize that they can work things out and become more cohesive as compared to more disjointed through resolution of disagreements.
    -   The stepfamily begins to build its own traditions and history.

The consistency between models seems to emphasize the assertion that time itself will not foster stepfamily cohesion and harmony. Rather than "wait and see," the key to a resolution of the identified developmental challenges is intentional awareness, negotiation, and effort on the part of all stepfamily members, including those who do not reside within the stepfamily home. For counselors, attention to these viewpoints, or others that may be proposed, and specific attention to the relevant stage tasks provide confirmation of possible challenges resolved and new issues to address. For stepfamily members, knowledge of these perspectives confirms the normalcy of their struggles and may reduce their bewilderment and feeling of defeat.

In summary, McGoldrick and Carter (2005) proclaimed that "so complex is the process of forming a remarried family that we have come to think of this process as adding a whole new phase to the family life cycle for those involved" (p. 417). The mainstream culture lacks any established patterns or rituals to help stepfamilies navigate their multifaceted relationships. In that void, dominant negative social discourses come to have a powerful influence on stepfamily members.

Issues of Diversity

In this section, I discuss what the professional literature has to say regarding developmental shifts as a function of the ethnicity or sexual identity of stepfamily members. The impact of culture on stepfamily dynamics is important to understand, which makes the paucity of research on families of color and gay and lesbian families all the more regrettable; in the words of Portrie and Hill (2005), "current research does not speak to the diversity and need for awareness of cultural issues" (p. 450). The situation has improved, but only slightly, since 2005; readers should not interpret this brevity of discussion as an indication of the lack of importance of this information but rather as an indication that scholarship is limited in this area. It is critical for the clinician and family members to honor the different life experiences of stepfamilies that represent the cultural diversity of the United States in the 21st century.

African American stepfamily dynamics are influenced by cultural definitions of (re)marriage, nonmarital childbearing, and definitions of family that include nonblood relationships. Cohabitation may be perceived as an alternative to marriage rather than prelude, which raises the possibility of cohabiting rather than married stepfamilies. The birth of children to unmarried women means that children may be present in a first marriage; a biological second parent might not be part of the picture. *Fictive kin* are valued family members whose connection is based on an emotional bond, willingness to help, and an enduring relationship but not on legal ties or obligations nor family lineage. This type of relationship expresses itself in more fluid family boundaries and experiences of the children of adults coming and going in their lives.

As I was writing this chapter, I was constantly stymied in my attempt to find any information specific to Hispanic stepfamilies. This lack of professional resources may indicate a challenge in identifying such families; issues of funding for their study; or reluctance among these families themselves to come to the notice of social service agencies, counselors, and family practitioners. Whether the presented models of stepfamily development and the issues germane to other cultural groups do indeed apply to Hispanic stepfamilies has yet to be determined.

Gay and lesbian stepfamilies are frequently paired and discussed as a unit in the few studies I was able to identify that dealt with these families. For consistency with the literature, I will discuss these two groups together; clinicians will have to rely on gay or lesbian stepfamily members to inform them as to which details are indeed relevant, and which are nonapplicable, to their life experiences as stepfamily members. Here, I present overarching themes unique to gay and lesbian stepfamilies as compared to stepfamilies from any other cultural group.

McGoldrick and Carter (2005) described the burdens of secrecy and isolation caused by the dominant social discourses fostering a negative social stigma concerning three related disclosures: one's sexual identity, one's partnership status, and one's parental role. Gay and lesbian stepfamilies must confront the anxiety about consequences of "coming out" in declaration of any or all three revelations, with no certainty of how these declarations may be received by friends, family, or social institutions. These three relational systems are intentionally listed based on issues of familiarity and possible social support. While the disclosure process to family and friends may be a single event, gay and lesbian stepfamilies will repeatedly confront possible social negation, if not prejudice, in interactions with employers, the legal system, schools, and faith-based establishments. In each case, varying degrees of acceptance or tolerance may be expected, with little recourse when faced with negative responses, so gay and lesbian stepfamilies seem to be faced with an ongoing dilemma: disclosure in hopes of acceptance but with fears of rejection or to remain secretive and isolated and without possible needed support. Therefore, the process of coming to terms with issues of sexual identity fold into the stages and system dynamics of blended and developing families.

A decade ago, Portrie and Hill (2005) criticized this paucity of professional knowledge, stating that "the limited multicultural research on blended families demands future research endeavors" (p. 450). It is regrettable that, 10 years later, the situation has not significantly changed.

Implications for Treatment Planning and Delivery

In summary, and as a launching platform for this section, perhaps developmental theory identifies common need while narrative therapy emphasizes the individual interpretation of that need. Applying the idea of turning points (Baxter et al., 1999), clinicians and family members can focus on pathways of relationship development and on nodal events, such as changes in household/family composition, conflict or disagreement, holidays or special events, quality time, family crisis, and reconciliation and problem solving—in other words, on transformative events that fostered a sense of family. Seen as "a framework that holds relevance for all blended families" (p. 293), these descriptive models can offer a new perspective for family members bogged down in what seems to be endless conflict.

The narrative integration asks each family member to share perspectives on the same event, coupled with consideration of social narratives around the same event. That very exploration uncovers for the family members the bewildering number of views of the same incident and how the differing reactions of family members make sense, given the perspectives that each holds. Given the myriad perspectives internal to the family and external from social narratives, it is no wonder that the family could not resolve that specific issue. Given that concentrated family resources can address any concern, the fragmentation of effort based on these views defeats the best efforts from any one family member. Rather it is the consensus of the family issue—through reauthoring that event, possible solutions, and possible contributions of each family member to the family's overall success—that will get "unstuck" the family specific to that presenting problem and, more generically, provide a new orientation to other and future family complaints and challenges.

McGoldrick and Carter (2011) provided a series of turning points for clinicians and family members to address. First, they recommended the utilization of the three-generational genograms to illustrate presenting or existing family patterns in the family of origin, the predivorce family, the single-parent family, and finally, the stepfamily. Just enumerating the four family constellations, doubled by the life experiences of each present spouse, confirms the foundational belief systems that each spouse brings to the final and current stepfamily life experiences. This exercise will allow the adults to recognize the differing expectations and practices based on those assumptions that each has accumulated over his or her relational history. Those insights might encourage a willingness to acknowledge the insufficiency of either prior belief system in addressing stepfamily developmental needs, with the resulting conjoint decision to reimagine how to create the type of stepfamily both imagine. McGoldrick and Carter recommended attention to nine critical areas where spouses' narratives and dominant social perspectives hold the potential for derailing a positive development of the new stepfamily.

1. Educating and normalizing patterns and processes in remarriage and "refamily/ing" bearing in mind that family members are at differing life cycles;
2. Exploring the emotionally central role of women (stepmothers) and the difficulty in moving into a new system where much is demanded of them and the emotionally distant role of men (stepfathers) and what is realistic for them;
3. Discouraging couples from trying to maintain the myth of the intact nuclear family;
4. Recreating the unrealistic ideals of remarriage;
5. Practicing patience for the ambiguity of guilt, divided loyalties, ambivalence, etc., among the children and stepchildren;

6. Discovering a positive way to involve ex-spouses and absent parents in sessions;
7. Resolving the feelings of loss for the closeness of the pre-stepfamily single-parent child relationship;
8. Building cooperative sessions to resolve a child's difficulties, as children never have the power to decide on remarriage, custody, or visitation; and;
9. Putting biological parents in charge of child uproar, with stepparent as observer and then co-coach.

These topics recur at each stage of stepfamily development, with positive, conjoint resolution practices serving to resolve each issue more smoothly and cooperatively with increased practice and competence.

Conclusion

There are advantages to the use of developmental theory when thinking about stepfamilies, but Baxter et al. (1999) identified four reasons to use developmental theory cautiously in this context. They expressed a concern that reliance on one developmental model may come at the expense of other important areas of focus, such as spousal, parental, and stepparental systems, as well as ex-spouses and ex-grandparents. Second, developmental models assume a linear progress through tasks, which may be inconsistent with life demands and changes. Third, these models provide little etiology for the stage tasks, leaving readers and practitioners to ponder the "why now?" with little guidance. Finally, the stage descriptions are not as discrete in real life as they are on paper, and to date, little empirical validation of the schemas is available. While anecdotal and qualitative reports confirm their accuracy and utility, no empirical substantiations could be located in the professional literature.

Nevertheless, developmental theory is an attractive framework to explain and normalize a family phenomenon. For the clinician, this orientation transcends episodes in favor of family patterns and replaces attention to complaints with a focus on task accomplishment. Portrie and Hill (2005) cautioned that "relying on assumptions about blended families may perpetuate cultural beliefs that endorse a deficit perspective of stepfamily functioning" (p. 445), but their judicious application may legitimize what has been viewed as toxic and pathological. Using the tenets of narrative therapy, "the key that determines whether a crisis is transitional or has permanent crippling impact is whether it is handled adequately within the family system, in spite of a general lack of social support offered by our society" (McGoldrick & Carter, 2011, p. 317). Awareness of developmental stages and tasks specific to stepfamily life may assist in the adequate handling "within the family system" as these authors observed. In addition, the lack of social support, or invalid existing social support, isolates stepfamilies, causing them to serve as their own support system and depriving them of external normalization of stepfamily progress. In other cases, the social support systems are proving unsupportive, lending credence to Stewart's remark (2007) that "very few have investigated the role that our social institutions might play with respect to these processes" (p. 51). This oversight supports a review of the roles of stepfamily members as defined and affected by social narratives. This exploration allows family members to become aware of how dominant narratives interfere with the resolution of specific stage tasks and to begin to reauthor those narratives in a manner more representative of lived stepfamily experience and more facilitative toward stage task resolution.

Resources

Anonymous. (n.d.) *The gay or lesbian stepparent*. Family Education. Retrieved from http://life.familyeducation.com/stepfamilies/sexuality/47611.html

The strengths and challenges of gay stepparenting

Missouri Families. (2009). *Stages of stepfamily development*. Missouri Families. Retrieved from http://www.missourifamilies.org/features/divorcearticles/divorcefeature42.htm

A summary of a five-phase model of stepfamily evolution

Papernow, P. (1989). *Seven stages of development for stepfamilies*. Stepfamily Association of America. Retrieved from http://www.home.comcast.net/~ndzimmer/stepfamily/stages.html

An overview of the phases of stepfamily development

Whiteside, M. F., & Campbell, P. (1993). *Stepparenting in gay and lesbian families: Integrity, safety, and the real world out there*. National Stepfamily Resource Center. Retrieved from http://www.stepfamilies.info/articles/stepparenting-in-gay-and-lesbian-families.php

A short description of the social challenges of stepparenting and sexual identity issues.

Chapter 3

Marital Issues in Stepfamilies

Stepfamily, stepparent, and *stepchild* are all terms and relationships that come to mind when the prefix *step* is applied to a family constellation. However, conspicuously absent from that list of pertinent expressions and affiliations is any direct reference to the marriage that has created the stepfamily unit itself (Jensen, Lombardi, & Larson, 2015; McGoldrick & Carter, 2011). It may appear that, once the wedding or ceremony of commitment is completed, attention to that family dynamic becomes less important than the issues relating to stepparenting (e.g., the increased complexity of two sets of stepchildren plus the addition of a mutual child) or resolving the multiple relational connections implicit in the formation of the stepfamily (American Psychological Association, 2013; Long & Young, 2007; Taylor & Taylor, 2012). Although parenting concerns are more immediate in terms of stepfamily adjustment, they must, at some point, be balanced with attention to the quality of the spousal relationship to facilitate stepfamily sustainability (American Psychological Association, 2013; Martin-Uzzi & Duval-Tsioles, 2013). Given the rates of divorce, remarriage, and second divorces in the United States today, understanding the couple relationship in stepfamilies is a critical component of understanding stepfamily success.

Remarriage Rates and Stepfamily Formation

Goldenberg and Goldenberg (2002) observed that Americans hold "an inherent marriage bias" (p. 165); they divorce and remarry at greater rates than people in most other countries (Lewis & Kreider, 2015). On average, men wait 2.3 years between divorce and remarriage, and women wait 2.5 years. Saint-Jacques et al. (2011) found that 66% of women and 75% of divorced men will remarry; according to Martin-Uzzi and Duval-Tsioles (2013), 30% remarry only 1 year after they divorce.

Approximately 65% of remarriages create a stepfamily (Jensen, Lombardi, & Larson, 2015; Schramm & Adler-Baeder, 2012). Deal (2014) hypothesized that 39% of White couples with children are stepcouples; so too are 55% of Black couples and 36% of Hispanic couples, leading to the assertion that stepfamilies are becoming one of the most common family forms in the United States (American Psychological Association, 2013). As of 1996, the U.S. government stopped tracking marriages, divorces, remarriages, and stepfamilies, and state-issued marriage licenses no longer ask about prior marriages. Therefore, nongovernmental sources are relied on for this information on a national or state level (see, e.g., Centers for Disease Control and Prevention, 1998).

Deal (2012, 2014) cited divorce rates of 67% for second marriages and 73% for third marriages, attributing this dissolution rate to high stress in stepfamilies during the first 5 years. That marital stress, according to Crosbie-Burnett and McClintic (2000), forces a reorganization of roles and relationships and perhaps even a displacement of an older child as the emotional support and confidant of the biological parent; it is possible that family members may not share the same understanding of the new relationships. (Deal also discovered that, over time, stress levels in stepfamilies can fall to levels consistent with first marriages.)

High remarriage rates among divorced persons suggest an optimistic belief that the next spouse and marriage will prove more satisfying than the previous one. Unfortunately, there is little research to support or disprove this belief; Martin-Uzzi and Duval-Tsioles (2013) found that "the majority of literature [focuses on] on stepparenting and blending of two families" (p. 43), rather than on the development of a satisfying marital relationship in the new stepfamily; Deal (2014) reached the same conclusion ("little research conducted on this topic"; p. 548). These findings suggest that couples may have little guidance on how to develop and maintain a healthy and nurturing marital relationship—the whole goal of remarriage.

Reasons for Stepfamily Marriages

"All couples, whether in stepfamilies or not, go through difficult moments" (Saint-Jacques et al., 2011, p. 549). However, in theories of marital development specific to first marriages, the quality of the marital relationship is predictive of the quality of the parenting, at least within nuclear family systems; an assumption is made that the newly married couple have time and energy to dedicate to the fledgling relationship prior to the arrival of children, an assumption that cannot be made for couples in stepfamilies. In any case, the role of parenting eventually diminishes as children mature and leave home. This raises the question: How can the spousal relationship be created and nurtured through the turmoil and confusion of stepfamily life (American Psychological Association, 2013; Ferrer, 2012)?

The turmoil and pain of divorce notwithstanding, the majority of divorced individuals remarry relatively quickly (i.e., within less than 3 years). The anticipated rewards of recoupling fall into two categories: spousal benefits and benefits to the children. Goldenberg and Goldenberg (2002) described the remarriage as holding the potential to rebuild self-esteem (i.e., that one is loving and worthy of love). If the adults have learned from their failed marriages, they may approach the second marriage more wisely and maturely, leading to a more stable relationship. Long and Young (2007) spoke of five potential motivators for remarriage, three of which are exclusively related to the spousal relationship: companionship, partnership, and sexual relations. (Two other motivators are arguably child-related: economic gains and a relief from single-parenting responsibilities.)

In theory at least, remarriage offers the possibility that children will be able to experience positive and mutually enhancing interactions between adults (Goldenberg & Goldenberg, 2002). A successful remarriage establishes children's trust in marriage and family (Taylor & Taylor, 2012). A successful remarriage offers children a sense of well-being and security as well as access to positive adult role models in a caring relationship (Ferrer, 2012). These considerations can be powerful motivators for single parents considering remarriage.

The Experiences of Spouses in Stepfamilies

Although stepfamilies are the fastest growing family unit in the United States today, "relatively little knowledge has institutionalized their transition and challenges as compared to first-marriage coupling" (Taylor & Taylor, 2012; see also Jensen, Lombardi, & Larson, 2015; Long & Young, 2007).

The adaptive challenges facing first-married couples apply to stepfamily couples. McGoldrick (2005) listed some of the normative early-marriage tasks: (a) resolving economic issues such as handling income, debt, and previous obligations; (b) addressing emotional issues including communication, intimacy, and dependence; (c) settling power arrangements such as issues of privilege to partnership and equity; (d) addressing physical power on the continuum from intimacy to abuse, from threats to belief in the sanctity of the individual; (e) establishing boundaries around the couple in relation to all other relationships and whether these boundaries are rigid, diffuse, or flexible; (f) navigating sexuality covering the continuum from sexual intimacy to sexual objectification and exploitation; and (g) handling chores and leisure time from priorities for caring for the home, responsibilities, and individual and conjoint leisure activities. In addition to these nontrivial negotiations and accommodations, stepfamily couples also must deal with at least three additional issues that significantly impinge on the quality, adaptability, and sustainability of the stepfamily couple: (a) the number of preexisting extramarital relationships that must be negotiated; (b) immediate parenting and stepparenting stress; and (c) the depleted reserves of time and energy available to dedicate to the satisfaction of the stepfamily marriage (Adler-Baeder, Robertson, & Schramm, 2010; Higginbotham & Agee, 2013; Schramm & Adler-Baeder, 2012). Each spouse brings a complete set of expectations and beliefs around each marital issue, but simply dealing with daily activities leaves little time for the couple to address together potentially divisive issues.

One of the tasks of first-married couples is to establish boundaries around the new spousal system and to negotiate priorities with family members and in-laws on such diverse issues as visiting, celebrating traditions, family versus nuclear-family togetherness time, and spiritual expressions. This may seem like a manageable list, but its complexity multiplies severalfold with the added "cast of characters" (Long & Young, 2007, p. 300) in typical stepfamily constellations—ex-spouses (perhaps with new partners of their own), children (residential and visiting), former in-laws, current in-laws, several sets of grandparents, and old friends. This is frequently daunting even for first-marrieds; consider, then, how much more complicated it might be in stepfamily marriages, where residual anger, resentment, and disappointment between former spouses may interfere with productive and cooperative communication around the number of daily issues demanding attention. Long and Young (2007) summarized this situation by stating that the "couple does not have time to establish a separate identity before dealing with these other people. . . . rarely is the time to build a strong foundation to support the remarriage available before the couple is involved with the challenges of stepfamily formation" (p. 302). Extrafamilial relationships may interfere with the building of a solid spousal union, and intrafamilial relationship may further distract the new spouses from the tasks of effective coupling.

Being a child in a new stepfamily is obviously different than in a first marriage where children have no "say" in who will parent them (Jensen, Lombardi, & Larson, 2015). The stepchild already holds an emotional bond with one parent over the other, while in first marriages, the child bonds differently but equally with both parents. The stepchild tends to have had "alone time" with one biological parent in the time between the dissolution of the first marriage and the remarriage, while, for the first-marriage child, the spousal bond was present from his or her birth. In addition, among children in first marriages, there is no absent parent figure with whom the child may share history and emotional connection, so, for children in first marriages, the spousal union is simply a fact of life; in existence prior to his or her arrival, the parameters and functioning of which are expanded with the parenting roles and duties. Children may prefer their living situation before the remarriage, when they did not have to share their parent. They may also feel displaced by the addition of stepsiblings into the family constellation, and they may resent the need to revise long-standing familiar traditions and rituals to accommodate the experiences and expectations of the stepparent. Children may view the stepparent as a major impediment to their dream of seeing their biological parents reconciled, and they may try to sabotage the new marriage (Ferrer, 2012; Taylor & Taylor, 2012).

Marital quality has been identified as foundational to the stepfamily success, both in addressing the extrafamilial relationships and intrafamilial challenges (Adler-Baeder, Robertson, & Schramm, 2010; Jensen, Lombardi, & Larson, 2015; Schramm & Adler-Baeder, 2012). Thus, it is disturbing to find delayed attention to marriage in favor of attention to the immediacy of the other relational obligations (Taylor & Taylor, 2012), priorities that seem to be based on the myths about coupling in stepfamilies. Higginbotham and Agee (2013) found that beliefs in stepfamily myths were negatively correlated with marital, personal, family, and life satisfaction for women and negatively correlated with parental satisfaction for men. Halford et al. (2007) attributed the higher divorce rate among stepfamilies to avoidance of difficult topics (more than occurs among first-married couples), accompanied by more spousal withdrawal, both factors reflective of a "function of uncertainty about the status and future of the marital relationship" (p. 480). Schrodt, Soliz, and Braithwaite (2008) reported similar results and speculated that mental health professionals would do well to help stepfamily couples explore the etiology of communication barriers and work to differentiate them from family-of-origin and first-marriage patterns.

In summary, researchers (Deal, 2014; Joanides, 2012; Martin-Uzzi & Duval-Tsioles, 2013; McGoldrick & Carter, 2011) have agreed that couples in stepfamilies are faced with two dilemmas: (a) They must navigate the unique challenges faced by stepfamilies without guidance, and (b) they must deal with "society's failure to differentiate being a spouse from stepparenting issues" (McGoldrick & Carter, 2011, p. 324). Society still does not recognize this family form as "normal," and the process of forming a stepfamily is not well understood (Higginbotham & Agee, 2013; McGoldrick & Carter, 2005). Higginbotham and Agee also concurred with Saint-Jacques et al. (2011), who stated that "one explanation for these difficulties relates to cognitive processes that may lead to distorted conceptions of stepfamily life" (p. 551). In the section that follows, I explore some of those "cognitive distortions."

Dominant Social Myths About Stepfamily Couples

Myth #1: The Wedding Will Lead to Mutual Love and Care

Spouses-to-be hope that because they are so enamored with one another, the new marriage will compensate for all the deficiencies of the preceding failed marital union and that they will not allow past ills or ongoing commitments to distract them from the new union. The stakes are high: Any blemish within the new idealized family confirms that this second spouse is also not "the one" and that perhaps it is time to cut one's losses and end this marriage.

Myth #2: The Marriage Will Compete With the Legacy of the Previous One

People commonly believe that the key to a more satisfying second marriage lies in finding the right partner rather than achieving better self-understanding. After all, it is the other party who is truly to blame for the failure of the first marriage, and a better choice of spouse should lead to success. Both parties carry with them the memories of their failed first marriages plus an idealized first-marriage template.

Myth #3: Everything Will Fall Into Place

People often retain an idealized understanding of marriage as something that happens spontaneously. Partners might expect the "magic" of courtship infatuation and the wedding to extend effortlessly into the marriage; if it does not, the reason must be that the partner is unsuitable. To succeed might require overlooking differences in values, habits, and preferences and to assume that, over time, those areas of potential conflict will somehow disappear and the spouses will agree on all matters of family life.

Myth #4: The Children Will Be Happy About the Remarriage

Because the biological parent is happy about the new marriage, the children will be too; they will welcome the new adult in their lives, if not for their own sakes, then for the sake of the parent who is clearly happier.

Myth #5: The Marriage Will Take Care of Itself, Focus on the Children

Given both the belief that things will (magically) fall into place and the needs of the children, some people believe that establishing a sound stepparent role is critical to family transition and adaptation and to managing levels of tension and potential conflict. A "good" parent will prioritize the needs of the children over those of the spouse who, as an adult, can understand why this is necessary. Giving priority to the needs of the children might be seen as necessary to counter the long-term impacts of the dissolved marriage and the period of single parenthood plus any ongoing conflict with the ex-spouse; the new family arrangement must serve as a buffer for the children from both their pasts and ongoing present traumas.

Narratives: Couples Describe Their Marital Issues

I had no idea that marriage in a blended family would be so different than my first marriage. It's just so much more complex. I wish someone would have told me this before we married.
—"Jane," Mother of two, stepmother of three, (2013)

So many couples in blended families divorce. How can I make sure this marriage is my last?
—Anonymous contributor, blog, (2013)

Malia and I have two children of hers and one of ours. We both work out of the home and weekends are spent getting the house in order, running errands, and attending to parenting events with the children. I have complained to her that we do not seem to have any fun with each other. All she says is that she is too tired and that she hopes in a few years, when the children are older, that we will have more time together as a couple.
—Derek, 2013

These comments support the literature regarding the puzzlement and lack of direction experienced by stepfamily couples. Such feelings of helplessness and hopelessness could possibly explain the dissolution rate of stepfamily couples. A lack of understanding of the normative nature of such experiences could cause the couple to doubt the strength of their marriage and, lacking guidance or focus, could internalize that disappointment and frustration. However, perhaps the initial intervention to prevent such a destructive cycle of disappointment, surrender, and divorce lies in the reconstruction of the myths that seem to underlie the couple's misconceptions about their remarriage (Ferrer, 2012; Higgenbotham & Agee, 2013; Long & Young, 2007; Taylor & Taylor, 2012).

Myth Reconstruction and Implications

"Without clear expectations of what is needed or expected in such a role, family members cannot employ available coping skills, solutions to problems are less easily reached and the situation is more likely to be felt as a crisis" (Goldenberg & Goldenberg, 2002, p. 181). Therefore, "having realistic expectations are critical for healthy stepfamily functioning" (Adler-Baeder, Robertson, & Schramm, 2010, p. 307; Ferrer, 2012; Long & Young, 2007). Stepcouples may be overly influenced by societal norms that consider the nuclear family as ideal yet, for the stepfamily, unrealistic. Critical attention must be paid to these "unconscious organizing principles" (Martin-Uzzi & Duval-Tsioles, 2013, p. 46), as these beliefs form the cognitive context in which individuals evaluate their situation, conduct themselves, and expect to be regarded by others. These assertions then authenticate the need for the reauthoring of the myths around being a "stepcouple."

Myth #1: The Wedding Will Lead to Mutual Love and Care

Myth Reauthoring

Ideally, the wedding may be a joyous ceremony, but in reality, this rite paves the road to a challenging marriage. Stepfamily life diminishes the importance of the marriage, and care must be taken to maintain its primacy and vibrancy. The fragility of the spousal union must be balanced with issues of stepparenting, which are both part and parcel of being an adult in the stepfamily but can never substitute for each other.

Implications for Effective Stepmarriages

Couples need to understand how marriages in stepfamilies differ from first marriages and to appreciate the expanded list of marital tasks that include, but go beyond, those of a first marriage. Discussions about how to honor one another need to take place prior to the wedding, so that the anticipation of this challenge is not overwhelmed by the immediacy of stepparenting. Only 25% of couples who anticipate forming a stepfamily seek premarital counseling (Deal, 2014). Lucier-Greer, Adler-Baeder, Ketring, Harcourt, and Smith (2012) advocated stepfamily-specific couples relationship education because they believed that stepfamily marital quality is a function of individual, relational, and parental functioning. Given the higher levels of marital instability, tension, disagreement, and open criticism that tend to exist in remarried families during the formative first 5 years, directed intervention specific to the needs of stepfamily

31

couples could provide strategies to understand, negotiate, and resolve the inevitable tensions that emerge.

Myth #2: The Marriage Will Compete With the Legacy of the Previous One

Myth Reauthoring

One marriage cannot compensate for the failures of a previous one, not without the partners involved being more insightful than they once were. Understanding the strengths and limitations of the first marriage are critical in understanding how to form a more successful relationship in the second union.

Implications for Effective Stepmarriages

The myth seems to be premised on two related yet separate assumptions: that issues from the first marriage will resolve themselves through the second union and that the stepfamily marriage is similar to first marriages. The first assumption is blatantly false; one must rationally and objectively evaluate one's own strengths, blind spots, and spousal style and then choose how to behave in the relationship. The second assumption is equally misguided; clearly, the complexity of the challenges of the stepfamily couple exceeds that of first-marrieds and challenges what one understands of normative marriage.

Myth #3: Everything Will Fall Into Place

Myth Reauthoring

In fact, one might conclude just as rationally that "everything will fall to pieces." There is no guarantee or automatic assurance that marriage will succeed, regardless of family constellation. Time and dedicated effort are required to make any marriage succeed, and that is doubly true of marriages that face the challenges of stepfamilies.

Implications for Effective Stepmarriages

Stepfamily marriages need special attention to succeed because family members might act either intentionally or haphazardly to weaken the marital bond. Stepchildren's demands may seem endless and their divided loyalty heartbreaking, and conflict with ex-spouses may seem trivial yet endless; unfortunately, these ongoing relational dynamics are normative aspects of stepfamily life. Therefore, only the couple can prioritize the stepfamily marriage. How couples decide to assume this onerous responsibility in the face of seemingly endless opposition provides the topics for directed discussion. No one else in the stepfamily constellation may be in any way committed to the success of the marriage, so if the couple are unable to work together on the quality and sustainability of their marriage, then, truly, "the pieces will fall apart."

Myth #4: The Children Will Be Happy About the Remarriage

Myth Reauthoring

At best, some of the children will be happy about the remarriage some of the time; the adults cannot expect all of the children to be supportive of the marriage all of the time, and they should not regard the children as allies in the task of creating a sustainable stepfamily marriage. Their presence and historical connections to biological spouses are established dynamics, and they may wish for their biological parent's happiness, but they are children, and thus their altruistic caring can be best described as inconsistent and based on self-interest.

Implications for Effective Stepmarriages

In first marriages, the responsibility for the quality of the spousal relationship lies, obviously, with the adults. Any reliance on the children to contribute to the marital quality is misguided. Although the children may appreciate the relative stability and tranquility of the remarriage, especially if the first marriage was conflict ridden and tension filled; the majority of their interactional efforts are self-serving. Children may hold no malice toward the new marriage or the stepparent, but neither will they facilitate its success merely for its own sake. Therefore, regardless of how supportive the children may have been during the courtship phase and how tired they might be of providing emotional support to their single parent, they may not welcome the stepparent into their lives.

Myth #5: The Marriage Will Take Care of Itself, Focus on the Children

Myth Reauthoring

No marriage "takes care of itself"; it requires effort and attention because competing demands are always present. In the stepfamily, the stepparent/ stepchild relationship is predictive of marital sustainability (Taylor & Taylor, 2012). However, the quality of the marital relationship serves as a buffer from stepparenting stress and the stepchildren's attempts to ally with the biological parent against the new stepparent.

Implications For Effective Stepmarriages

Although the needs of the children should never be overlooked (nor are children likely to accept second-place status), the couple must acknowledge two equally important priorities that deserve attention. This balance is harder to achieve in a stepfamily than in a first marriage, because the couple has time prior to the arrival of children to cement the marital relationship. The uniqueness of this challenge is normative to all stepfamily couples and couples need to understand that there is a positive correlation between the time dedicated to the marriage and the satisfaction level reported by each partner (Martin-Uzzi & Duval-Tsioles, 2013).

Issues of Cultural Diversity and Stepfamily Marriages

Research specific to the diverse needs of stepfamily couples offered some interesting perspectives. As noted, research has tended to focus on stepparent issues and not issues related to stepfamily couples. This suggests that two assumptions are being made: that the marital tasks take second place to parenting issues and that the couple relationship will somehow survive and thrive. This section presents what is known about the issues faced by African American, gay, and lesbian stepfamily couples. (Hispanic stepfamily couples are not discussed, because a literature search conducted in Spring 2015 did not yield published studies on this group.)

Stewart (2007) reported that African American stepfamily couples indicated lower qualities of marital satisfaction. Spouses tend to rate the behavior of one another more negatively than do White stepfamily spouses. They assessed their disagreements and conflict management at levels comparable to those of White stepfamily couples but rated their overall relational happiness as lower. These findings may be attributable to differing expectations or to differing assessments of marital skills. African American stepfamily couples may have to deal with extended family interference to a greater extent than do White stepfamily couples. This dynamic may reflect deprioritization of the stepfamily spouse, most often a stepfather, as a temporary family presence in comparison to the preexisting biological and fictive kin network. In addition, stepfamily spouses tend to be younger than among the White stepfamily community, with fewer developed coping skills and less of a peer social support network. Given these dynamics, the obstacles to the sustainability of the stepfamily couple among this community seem daunting.

The issues faced by gay and lesbian stepfamily couples are similar. Skogrand, Mendez, and Higginbotham (2013) reported that 30% of lesbian couples and 17% of gay couples describe themselves as a "stepfamily" and face issues that are "comparable to heterosexual stepfamilies" (see also Van Eeden-Moorefield, Pasley, Crosbie-Burnett, & King, 2012). These couples face three important additional stressors. The first revolves around the lack of social recognition and legal status for these families (Leland, 2014), although this is changing and increasing numbers of states are introducing ballot initiatives to recognize same sex unions. The second issue unique to these couples is the relationship with extended family members, which is a function of the degree of acceptance of one's sexual orientation by one's family-of-origin and by one's larger social network. This degree of "out-ness" has been identified as a critical dynamic between partners. Often this notion of a covert sexual identity is caused by concerns about child custody or visitation and other issues remaining from the dissolved heterosexual relationship in which the children were born and over which the legal system, with its varying degrees of acceptance of gay and lesbian relationships still holds a powerful decision-making authority. The third issue may arise as members of the couple are at differing stages of accepting and expressing their same-sex orientation (Stewart, 2007).

Conclusion

In summary, remarriages are nearly as common as first marriages, albeit more complex and challenging than first marriages (Goldenberg & Goldenberg, 2002; Long & Young, 2007). In both first and subsequent marriages, strengthening the spousal relationship remains a critical task (Jensen, Lombardi, & Larson, 2015). Adler-Baeder, Robertson, and Schramm (2010) discovered there are few models of success but not as prevalent or as popular as those pertaining to nuclear family spousal functioning. Higginbotham and Agee (2013) argued that the field of counseling needs to focus on "identifying and establishing functional standards for their remarriages and stepfamilies" (p. 188); this requires "longitudinal studies, with more diverse samples, that would further the field's understanding of the role re-marital cognitions and consistency play in perceived adjustment over time" (p. 189). Continued work in this area holds the promise of "establishing reliable, predictive models of marital quality unique to stepfamily couples" (Schramm & Adler-Baeder, 2012, p. 1393).

Resources

Anonymous. (2010). *Stepfamily problems don't have to end in divorce.* Happy Together Forever. Retrieved from http://happytogetherforever.com/stepfamily-problems-dont-have-to-end-in-divorce/

Common stepfamily challenges and behavioral strategies to resolve these normative challenges within the stepfamily marriage

Bliss, B. (n.d.). *Step families.* Parenthood in America. Retrieved from http://parenthood.library.wisc.edu/Bliss/Bliss.html

Behavioral interventions for fostering stepfamily marital cohesion

Pasley, K. (1993). *What do we know about the marital relationship in stepfamilies?* National Stepfamily Resource Center. Retrieved from http://www.stepfamilies.info/articles/marital-relationship-in-stepfamilies.php

A summary of the dearth of understanding of successful stepfamily marriages and a call for clinical study research focusing on stepfamily marital successes and strengths

Pasley, K. (1995). *How first marriages can affect second marriage.* National Stepfamily Resource Center. Retrieved from http://www.stepfamilies.info/articles/how-first-marriages-can-affect-second-marriages.php

An outline of intermarital patterns and challenges

Stepparenting

At first glance, a chapter on stepparenting might seem redundant in light of chapters devoted to the experiences, issues, and concerns of stepmothers and stepfathers. The focus on stepparenting is designed to call attention to the complexity and centrality of the role of the stepparent. Moreover, the attachment of the prefix *step* to a familial relationship denotes a legal standing, a fact that might be overlooked; people are more likely to think of *stepparent* in terms of emotional bonding or affiliation (Favez, Widner, Doan, & Tissot, 2015).

Becoming a parent is usually preceded by a 9-month period, during which one becomes mentally prepared to assume a new role. Parents-to-be can read the classic *What to Expect When You're Expecting* (Murkoff & Mazel, 2015), or they can seek the advice of mothers and grandmothers in how to prepare for the arrival of the new child. Then, as changing diapers is traded for teaching writing and spelling, a parent slowly develops a personal style regarding such things as how to give praise and to implement consequences and when to say no or yes. Parents develop their own parenting styles over time, yet individuals often feel that they become stepparents almost overnight (Bigner, 2006). No authoritative or instructive books on the subject are available, and even the advice of older relatives in stepfamilies may not be relevant to the situations that stepparents face today.

Other significant differences between the experience of a biological parent and a stepparent are worth identifying. The stepparent walks into a situation in which the child already has an established relationship with a parent; some precedents and understandings are already in place (Pace, Shafer, Jensen, & Larson, 2015). Stepparents are expected to parent with a set of rules already in place; these rules, formed by others, might not be acceptable to the stepparent (Shapiro & Stewart, 2012). Biological parents learn to respond to one child at a time before additional children are added to the family constellation, whereas stepparents must adapt immediately to at least one and often more than one child, each with differing needs and expectations. Finally, the children themselves must be regarded as actors: Children may be unwilling (or less than enthusiastic) participants in the stepfamily formation (Bigner, 2006). If the stepchildren are old enough to express themselves, then they have something to say about how their stepparents assume their roles. The acceptance and regard of the stepchildren is a critical factor in the acceptance of the new family structure in general and of the stepparent in particular (Shapiro & Stewart, 2012).

It is worth noting that a spouse in a stepfamily is not referred to as a *stepwife* or *stephusband*. That spouse is referred to specifically as *husband* or *wife* or more neutrally as *partner*. The very designation of the *step* label implies a special role, requiring singular attention. This chapter will describe and then deconstruct the myths around stepparenting and then move on to discuss research findings on four issues relevant to stepparenting: the age of the children in the stepfamily, confusion regarding the issues of stepparent discipline, appreciation of the issues of boundaries and loyalties in the stepfamily, and legal issues for stepparents.

The transition into the stepparenting role is neither immediate nor smooth (Favez, Widner, Doan, & Tissot, 2015; Felker et al., 2002; Martin-Uzzi & Duval-Tsioles, 2013; Shapiro & Stewart, 2012). The parental authorities of the biological parent and stepparent are confusing: The stepparent can exercise no more parental authority than the biological parent offers and the children accept. The right to stepparent must be earned and not demanded. Because there are few positive role models for the role of stepparent, each family must reimagine and enact the role on its own (Garneau & Adler-Baeder, 2015); there is little useful guidance on how to be an effective stepparent. For stepparents who do not have biological children of their own, the stepparent role becomes more challenging as they try to determine the "relational lens" they should use: pseudoparent, friend, disciplinarian, or some combination thereof. People who find themselves in the stepparent role are typically not prepared for the host of stepfamily issues they face, all of which require immediate resolution (Pace, Shafer, Jensen, & Larson, 2015); the following list provides a sample.

- Common stepchild discipline problems
- Conflicts over stepparent responsibilities and authority
- Custody, visitation, and/or financial support issues
- The disputes over parenting, money, privacy, vacations, responsibilities, boundaries, rituals, holidays, and so on
- Excessive guilt related to prior divorce or to re/marriage
- Feelings of being overwhelmed, confused, discouraged, "depressed," and self-doubting about their stepfamily situation
- Feelings of being used, ignored, unappreciated, and unsupported
- Hostility and/or aggression among coparents
- Intense loyalty conflicts
- Legal suits related to child custody changes

- Parenting differences over values and practices
- Stepchild behaviors like disrespect, "acting out," or "favoritism"
- Stepparent and ex-spouse jealousy issues
- Stepparent–stepchild rejections
- Stepsibling relationship problems
- The ways in which children act out and express their emotions

Schmeeckle (2007) studied the remembrances of adults who had acquired stepparents during their childhoods. About 86% of stepchildren reside with their biological mother and stepfather; the study tried to balance attention to stepmother and stepfather families. This qualitative study revealed differing patterns for stepmothers and for stepfathers. Respondents remembered that their stepmothers assumed the child care role even when the biological father was present. Not surprisingly, stepfathers deferred to the biological mother in this regard. Stepfathers seemed to provide instrumental support while stepmothers focused on *"kin-keeping"* (p. 179), or maintaining the multiple relationships that coincide with stepfamily formation. Stepfathers invested in the lives of stepchildren and biological children equally, but stepmothers were more invested with their biological children. Regardless of gender of child, stepfathers displayed more egalitarian parenting style than first-married fathers, possibly a reflection of time spent as a single parent. Stepchildren felt less emotional connection from stepmother as compared to biological children but still reported feeling close to her. The results are interesting because they demonstrate "some of the rich and gendered way stepparents and stepchildren are linked in families today" (p. 187).

Stepparenting Myths

Stepparenting, an "increasingly common parenting role" (Shapiro & Stewart, 2012, p. 833), is linked with increased stress and depression as a function of relational challenges with nonexistent directives and few, if any, positive role models or institutionalized frameworks for effective stepparenting. Yet "our culture promotes many stereotypical images of stepparents that are largely negative in nature" (Bigner, 2006, p. 245); these stereotypes receive wide expression through popular media venues and influence the thinking of stepfamily members and society at large. Some common myths about the roles played by stepparents are presented in the following sections.

Myth #1: The Stepparent as Rescuer

Stepparents might assume that they can compensate for the absent biological parent by "rescuing" the stepfamily. Perhaps one of the most notable "rescuers" was played by Julia Roberts in *Stepmom* (Columbus, 1998). In the film, Julia Roberts (the stepmother) sees herself as the "rescuer" of a father and his children as their mother is undergoing treatment for cancer. She engages with the family by completing tasks and doing kin-keeping their mother can no longer do. The children's biological mother, played by Susan Sarandon, feels threatened and intimidated by the rescuer role the stepmom is playing. When stepfathers play the rescuer role, they might provide financial stability for the wife and stepchildren. Variations of this narrative can be held by multiple members of the blended family.

Myth #2: The Stepparent as Super-Parent

Mike and Carol Brady (*The Brady Bunch*) seemed to be super-parents. The bonding with their stepchildren seemed effortless. Carol appeared to have little difficulty assuming the role of "mom" to the boys, and the same was true of Mike with the girls. Snap back to reality and we see that, while many stepparents desire to be super-parents, their ability to do so does not rely on them alone. The desire to be a super-parent can be easily fueled by the need to gain approval of the stepchildren or to receive some sort of external validation as a stepparent. The super-parent can also be a narrative developed by children in the blended family; they might see the stepparent as the giver of gifts during the courtship phase and as a fairytale character who will make their lives better.

Myth #3: The Stepparent as "Pal"

Many new stepparents are driven by the goal to bond with their step-children—to have their stepchildren "like" them. After all, in many cases, the custodial parent's opinion of the potential partner is divided between the attractiveness of that person and the receptivity of the children. As individuals begin the process of blending into a family, spouses and children alike might encourage the stepparent to adopt the role of a pal. This strengthens the perception that this approach to the new relationship is valid.

Myth #4: The Stepparent as Nonentity

Some stepfamilies completely overlook the parental role of the new stepparent. All power and authority continue to reside in the biological parent, and the stepparent functions much like a family guest—a presence but not an involved actor in the family. The single parent–children dynamics remain unchanged; the stepparent, at most, shares some to the household responsibilities.

Myth #5: The Stepparent as Equal to the Biological Parent

The stepparent might be expected to assume all of the family responsibilities once enacted by the same-gender biological parent who is now absent. The stepparent might be expected to exercise equal authority as the custodial parent and perhaps even be allocated spheres of authority apart from the biological parent. In addition, the stepparent might be seen as an equal parent if both adults have children from previous relationships; each may assume a tacit license to parent one's stepchildren as though they are one's biological parent.

Narratives: Stepparents Describe Their Lives

One of the most challenging and dynamic positions I have ever undertaken in my life is my role as a step-parent. Step-parenting can find some of its participants completely unprepared for the journey that lies before them. Taking on the joint responsibility of raising a child is not something one should take lightly. It is a huge responsibility that at times is not only challenging and intriguing, but can also be just as encouraging and rewarding in the long term.

—Retrieved from http://www.todaysmodernfamily.com/index. php/tag/blended-families-in-the-bible (10/28/2012)

Yet stepfathers today, unlike the past, get little respect. In fact, stories about "bad" stepfathers circulate so widely that a prominent sociologist and social commentator recently claimed that a woman with children who remarries is committing child abuse! This stunning misuse of social science research is based upon studies that lumped together boyfriends, uncles, grandfathers, and friends of the mother under the category of "stepfather" and found that such men were more likely than the biological father to abuse children. If we limit the category of "stepfather" to those men who have married the mother of their stepchildren, there is little difference between biological fathers and stepfathers in propensity toward child abuse.

—Retrieved from http://babybondingbookfordads.blogspot. com/2008/06/what-about-stepdads.html (06/03/2008)

I am living with my boyfriend. We have one son together, I have two daughters age 5 and 7 and he has 3 daughters 3, 6, 8. We have been together for almost 3 yrs. We have had countless fights regarding our children and parenting styles. I will admit, I at times get jealous of my boyfriend and his daughters relationship. He dotes over the little one to no end, treats her and talks to her like a baby, and does everything for her even though she can do most things herself.

—Retrieved from http://www.stepsforstepmothers.com/ pboard2.html (12/09/2012)

The bewilderment and confusion that confront stepparents, regardless of gender, and of intent, seem clear.

Myth Reconstruction and Implications

Bigner (2006) asserted that "the role of the stepparent is distinct from that of a biological parent" (p. 245). Furthermore, these dynamics are complicated by the preconceptions of what the role of stepparent "should" be. If the belief that the social world really is constructed through everyday talk is true (Kemp, Segal, & Robinson, 2013; Pace, Shafer, Jensen, & Larson, 2015), it would be useful to deconstruct the common myths about stepparenting and develop healthy and realistic alternatives. The first step in that process involves "giving up the dream or discarding unrealistic fantasies and ex-pectations of the new family system and its members" (Bigner, 2006, p. 249).

Reconstructing Myth #1: The Stepparent as Rescuer

The view that the stepfamily requires "rescuing" from either past parenting practices or hardships places the new stepparent in a one-dimensional role.

Moreover, continuity in that role is dependent on the continued dysfunction of the stepfamily: If the stepparent performs the rescuer role effectively, then he or she will have no contribution to make to the family. In addition, by defining the stepfamily role in terms of the needs of stepfamily members, the stepparent's personal roles are negated. This abrogation of personal need may lead to feelings of disgruntlement, underappreciation, and uncertainty about one's future in the stepfamily.

The most obvious reauthoring would be to see the stepparent as an additional resource to the stepfamily whose contribution must be balanced with an expectation of personal respect and attention. Stepparents should be asked to set a proactive agenda of "giving" rather than merely to respond to what is seen as lacking in the stepfamily. Ideally, this conversation and negotiation can precede creation of the stepfamily household so that both spouses and all concerned children can honor and enact this script.

Reconstructing Myth #2: The Stepparent as "Super-Parent"

The notion of a super-parent seems admirable until one considers the cost. Finding the right balance between attention to personal, spousal, and parental needs is optimal, yet "super-parenting" can only occur at the expense of other needs. Granted that occasions do arise when the demands of the parental role supersede all other roles, a balance must be struck if the stepparent is to function as a super-parent, providing nurturance and support without resentment or burnout.

The desire to prove one's parental worthiness may spur the drive to super-parent, but the stepparent should not overlook the equally important roles of adult and spouse. Ongoing communication with one's spouse about attending to the satisfaction within that relationship coupled with an honest assessment of one's sense of personal fulfillment will foster the needed balance of roles. It would seem critical that "super-parenting" be seen as a short-term intervention and not a permanent role.

Reconstructing Myth #3: The Stepparent as "Pal"

The stepparent may assume the role of "pal" at the request of the biological parent or because of a lack of desire to assume a parental role. Stepparents may be attempting to build rapport with the children; assuming the role of a pal might be thought to reduce the amount of conflict between them. However, if the stepparent role as pal is not mutually agreed upon, it can create conflict within the couple. Should the stepparent–pal become authoritative, children might feel confused or even betrayed. In addition, it would seem obvious that an adult in a home would hold adult responsibilities. Alliance with the children threatens the marital alliance and may cause the biological parent to wonder whether the spouse is, in fact, a parenting ally and support.

Because the stepparent is a stranger to the children, the distinctions between being "friendly" and a "friend" are important. Friendliness (an interest in the life of the child, a desire to help, being a source of support

42

and encouragement) is desirable to build positive relationships with any child. Being a friend (support at the expense of honesty, alliance against other adults, and perhaps endorsement of activities of which the parent might disapprove) is also a short-term means to build a connection with a child but will exact dire long-term consequences, such as conflict with the biological parent who had thought that the new adult would, in some fashion, be a parent and not a play-friend, and resentment by the children when the initial role becomes replaced with a more adult, perhaps parental, stance. Like any teacher or coach, the stepparent has lessons to impart to children with each interaction. The value of the stepparent in the eyes of the children may be a function of the value of those lessons, the kindness with which they are offered, the encouragement that accompanies them, and the successful results they bring about.

Reconstructing Myth #4: The Stepparent as Nonentity

Children may pretend that the stepparent does not exist because they prefer the familiarity of living only with the single parent or they secretly hope for a reconciliation between their biological parents. Pretending that the stepparent does not exist is disrespectful to the new adult and must be addressed by the biological parent.

Children do have a voice in how the family operates, but ultimately it is the adult who chooses the spouse. The biological parent must communicate clearly that he or she remains the "authority" but that the stepparent will be accorded the respect due any adult and that any rule enforcement by the stepparent will have the support of the biological parent. The biological parent must clearly communicate to the children that reconciliation with the absent biological parent is not possible and that the stepparent is in no way attempting to replace or displace that absent parent but rather to offer some new "gifts" (e.g., talents, skills) to the family. A wise stepparent takes an interest in the activities of the children, offering help where possible and demonstrating other abilities that might interest the children.

Reconstructing Myth #5: The Stepparent as Equal to the Biological Parent

For reasons of biology and familiarity, the stepparent will always hold a "one-down" position to the biological parent. This may be more difficult for the stepparent who is also a biological parent to accept. However, influence and affection may build over time if offered with patience and no expectation of return.

The role of the stepparent as a "one-down" parent or pal should be addressed prior to the formation of the stepfamily for many reasons, including its effect on a harried biological parent who is hoping that the stepparent will equally share child rearing responsibilities. However, both spouses need to understand the reality of the step situation and negotiate expressions of "separate" parental authority and mutual support. After the spouses jointly decide how to respond to a situation, each could serve as "principal" communicator to his or her biological children. This approach helps children to regard expectations and rules as characteristic of this family rather than as an arbitrary imposition from the new stepparent.

Issues Generic to Stepparenting

Adults in a first marriage may decide when and whether to have children, but stepparents have no such latitude in deciding when become a parent (Pace, Shafer, Jensen, & Larson, 2015). The challenge of parenting comes with the marriage, and four (sometimes overlapping) issues must be addressed (Bigner, 2006; Kemp et al., 2013; Stewart, 2007). The resolution of these issues determine the quality of stepfamily life and the experience of the stepparent (Garneau & Adler-Baeder, 2015).

Considerations of the Age/s of the Child/ren

Each stepfamily is unique, but all stepfamilies face common stepparenting issues (Berger, 2000). Bigner (2006) observed that "the problems and challenges facing stepfamilies are different from those of other family systems, especially when children are involved" (p. 238). Stepmothers and stepfathers come in to the role of stepparent with preconceived notions of who they should be and how they should act. Depending on their age, children can likewise bring a set of expectations.

Although much research has yet to be done on stepfamily development, some insights have been gleaned on the role of child age on stepfamily functioning. The literature is pretty conclusive that, in general, the younger the children are in a stepfamily, the better overall functioning will be (Bigner, 2006; Schrodt, 2006c; see also Gosselin & David, 2007). Schrodt reported that *bonded* stepfamily types tend to involve children who were younger when the stepfamily formed. One possible explanation for this is that younger children have had less exposure to social myths and, therefore, have fewer expectations of the new stepfamily, which leaves the stepfamily free to form on terms set by the parental unit. Older children often expect the stepparent to embody the best of the absent parent. Bigner (2006) noted:

> one of the disadvantages that challenge effective stepfamily formation is that the children involved frequently are adolescents (a finding supported by King, Boyd & Thorsen, 2015). Because of their developmental focus on individuation from their families, struggles can be expected when the adults involved demand their teenager's participation in activities that are aimed to develop a family identity."(pp. 242–244).

Kemp et al. (2013) offered the following guidelines:

> Children under 10:
> May adjust more easily as they desire cohesive family relationships
> Are more accepting of new adults
> Feel competitive for parental attention
> Have more daily needs to be met

Adolescents aged 10–14:
    May have most difficult time adjusting to stepfamily
    Need more time to bond before accepting step as disciplinarian
    May not demonstrate feelings openly but are sensitive to needing love, support, discipline, and attention
Teenagers 15 and over:
    May have less involvement in stepfamily life
    Prefer to separate from family to form individual identity
    Still wanting to feel important, loved, and secure within the stepfamily

King, Boyd, and Thorsen (2015) found that the quality of the mother–child relationship and the stepfather–stepchild relationship are two distinct barometers of adolescents' feelings of belonging and mattering in stepfamilies. For information about stepparent relations with grown, absent stepchildren and the impact of the new stepfamily formation on adult children, see Harris (2014).

Discipline

Like the nuclear family, the stepfamily functions best when both parents (biological and step) are regarded as authority figures. This does not imply equal authority, however. Schrodt (2006c) studied more than 500 stepchildren and found that:

> what primarily distinguished this most functional stepfamily type (*bonded*) from the other four types (*evasive, functional, ambivalent, and conflictual*) was the level of parental authority granted to the stepparent, which in turn corresponded with relatively high levels of positive regards for the stepparent and relatively low levels of dissension and avoidance among family members. (p. 321)

Schrodt (2006c) also found that a *functional* stepfamily type can occur when the stepparent is seen as more of a friend. What distinguishes a *functional* stepfamily type from that of a *bonded* stepfamily is that the level of stepparent authority is lower. However, the children in this stepfamily type still had "moderately high levels of positive regard" for their stepparent (p. 322). Schrodt concluded that stepfamily systems can still function quite well even if the stepparent is seen as friend. These allocations of authority are better based on need of the child as compared to being based on the wishes of the stepparent.

Boundaries and Loyalties

Issues of boundaries and loyalties in stepparenting seem to get more complicated the older children are at the time the stepfamily is formed. It can often be a confusing time for children who are old enough to cognitively process what is happening. Bigner (2006) noted that "it is not unusual for stepchildren to feel as if they are being pulled in several directions at once, which tests the strength of their personal boundaries" (p. 241). Schrodt and his colleagues (2008) also found in their review of the literature that "children may attempt to reconcile the stress and guilt associated with tri-angulation in family systems by aligning themselves more with one parent (typically the residential parent) than the other" (p. 213). Over time, this phenomenon paired with the reduced time a child might spend with the nonresidential parent can cause deterioration in the relationship.

A qualitative study of 60 French families showed that biological moth-ers had a significant amount of influence on the type and the quality of the relationship between her children and their new stepmother (Cadolle, 2000). In that study, mothers reported they did not want to coparent with the stepmother and were tired of her, thus creating loyalty difficulties for the children involved. Studies from the United States and Canada also support this notion that biological mothers can retain most, if not all, of the parenting responsibilities after a divorce. A similar study found that, while many dynamics affect the overall adjustment of adolescents in step-family systems, it is the relationship with the mother that is the strongest predicting variable (Saint-Jacques & Chamberland, 2000).

Legal Issues

The previous sections described issues and challenges that stepfamilies face with their own formation. However, stepfamilies also face unique challenges in the larger social systems of which they are a part, such as the legal system (Gold, 2009). Understanding the legal issues in stepparenting is of critical importance for family counselors. Moreover, this knowledge can be used to deconstruct legal "myths" a family might have. Three important areas will be addressed: the legal rights of parents and stepparents; finan-cial responsibility; and the rights of stepparents should the marriage end.

The law at both the federal and state levels is very clear that the rights of biological parents to raise and care for their children are exclusive. Gold's (2009) review of relevant case law determined that the laws "declare that a child cannot have more than two parents, each with full parental rights that are shared with no one else" (p. 273). Thus, unless a court determines otherwise, a stepparent is seen as a "legal stranger" to his or her stepchild. If biological parents are absent, stepparents are given legal rights to step-children, which occurs in one of the following ways:

- *In loco parentis* (Latin for "in place of a parent"): the law acknowledges stepparents as persons who "assume an active parental role and attach legal consequences to this voluntary behavior" (Mahoney, 2006, p. 100). An example of this might include a residential stepfather who is allowed under *in loco parentis* to put his stepchildren on his insurance but their nonresidential biological father still continues to pay child support. This practice of *in loco parentis* does not diminish the biological parent of their financial responsibility to the children (Gold, 2009).
- *De facto parenting* (Latin for "in fact"): the law acknowledges stepparents are "in fact" the parent of the child because they have assumed the role of biological parents in the absence of the real biological parent (Gold, 2009).

- *Adoption:* Adoption may occur for a *de facto* parent with the consent of the noncustodial parent or the termination of his or her rights by the court (Gold, 2009).

The financial responsibility of a stepparent is largely determined by their standing as far as the law is concerned. The majority of stepparents have legal standing as a "stranger" to their stepchildren, thus leaving them with no financial responsibility to their stepchildren (Gold, 2009). However, if a stepparent is serving *in loco parentis* and both biological parents relinquish their rights or are deceased, the stepparents could then be ordered by a court to provide support for the child. Exceptions to these guidelines include the codicils in the Higher Education Act of 1965 around issues of responsibility for college tuition plus more recent state laws that legislate family obligation. Clinicians must help stepfamily members be aware of changes and additions to the law to consider state law variations on these matters. Moreover, awareness of their presence does not substitute for sound legal counsel.

In the event of divorce, stepparent rights are, for the most part, nonexistent. As Gold noted (2009), "[s]tepparents hold no legal rights of custody or visitation but can petition if custody or access can be demonstrated to be in the best interests of the child" (p. 275). In most cases where custody was awarded to a stepparent, the nonresidential parent was not a part of the child's life and the stepparent was acting *in loco parentis* (Gold, 2009). In summary, current legal definitions of the rights and responsibilities of the stepparent continue to prioritize biology over physical presence and emotional bond. However, state laws are evolving to support the continuation of the parent–child relationship that forms between stepparents and children even after divorce.

Issues of Cultural Diversity and Stepparenting

It is of continued significance to this topic that the most recent literature search specific to the terms *African American, Hispanic, gay,* or *lesbian* with *stepparents* conducted in July 2013 revealed so few articles. While there were some dissertations listed regarding the perceptions of stepparenting among these groups, that search discovered only 3 articles pertaining to African American stepparenting, none specific to Hispanic stepparenting, 6 relevant to gay stepparenting, and 9 directly related to lesbian stepparenting, and, surprisingly, none of the articles appeared in the professional literature later than 2006. Two things are clear: Additional research is needed, and available sources must be used cautiously because many use small samples and are dated (Stewart, 2007).

African American stepfamilies reported were less likely to involve marriage and more likely to involve a nonmarital birth and cohabitation. Whether the adults were married, cohabiting, or separate, the family structure for the children was described as less rigid, with more permeable boundaries. Family membership is based as much on emotional bonds, a willingness to help, and enjoyable and enduring relationships, thereby perhaps providing the children with a wider array of stepparent figures than in remarried families. In addition, the children may "live" in several homes, based on needs and the capacity of the parent and caregivers. The understanding of family also may include a broader community and faith-based support system than is available to White stepfamilies. Children are reported as having to "face substantial societal disapproval" (Stewart, 2007, p. 151) in the multiple family homes with multiple fictive kin caregivers. There is also a distinction between biological father of the child and the man living in the home. In addition, the presence of extended family makes the role of new parent (especially stepfather) harder. Males are seen as temporary figures, with the stability and strength of the family centered in the female figures. In the absence of research, one might hypothesize that such a life experience would affect the role perceptions of the boys and girls raised within this environment in ways that would perpetuate this system.

Gay and lesbian stepparents seem to hold the same romantic ideals of stepfamily life as heterosexual stepparents (Stewart, 2007, p. 166). Like heterosexual stepfamilies, gay and lesbian stepfamilies experience confusion regarding the parenting hierarchy, the exclusivity of the biological parent–child connection, and the exclusion of the stepparent. However, gay and lesbian stepparents encounter and must deal with prejudicial social myths:

- Children may lack a safe refuge from pressures of living in a gay or lesbian household
- Disapproval from religious communities
- Fears that the children will become homosexual or adopt nontraditional gender roles
- Fears that the children will be sexually abused
- Fears that children will be stigmatized or emotionally traumatized
- Ridicule and rejection from peers, which may make children reluctant to invite friends to the house

Despite all the negative perceptions regarding children in gay or lesbian stepfamilies, Stewart's (2007) review of the literature revealed that, when these children are compared to children in heterosexual families, they are no worse off when assessed on specific mental health issues, behavior problems, self-concept, locus on control, intelligence, moral judgment, and peer relationships.

Conclusion

The stepparent role is often unclear yet essential in the functioning of the stepfamily (Garneau & Adler-Baeder, 2015; Martin-Uzzi & Duval-Tsioles, 2013; Pace, Shafer, Jensen, & Larson, 2015). A qualitative study of 15 couples revealed a consensus about role confusion, aspirations of parental equity which led to stress with the biological parent, deferring to the biological parent which led to resentment, and a culminating feeling of being undervalued and unable to fit in (Martin-Uzzi & Duval-Tsioles, 2013). Both step-fathers and stepmothers unanimously spoke of desiring a close relationship with the stepchildren, but they expressed confusion and uncertainty about how to accomplish this goal. Moreover, most stepparents sensed that their needs came last in terms of family priority, which suggests issues between the biological parents and stepparents that should be further studied and addressed. Further research is needed to "help all value and facilitate the stepparent-stepchild relationship as a means to address the stepparent's well-being as well as the child's" (Shapiro & Stewart, 2012, p. 837).

Resources

Deal, R. (2012). *Stepparenting do's and don'ts.* Family Life. Retrieved from http://www.familylife.com/articles/topics/parenting/stepparents/stepparenting-skills/stepparenting-discipline-dos-and-donts#

A list of suggestions for more purposeful and positive stepparenting

Pasley, K. (1994). *What is effective stepparenting?* National Stepfamily Resource Center. Retrieved from http://www.stepfamilies.info/articles/what-is-effective-stepparenting.php

Research-based interventions to support positive stepparenting

Pasley, K., Dollahite, D., & Ihinger-Tallman, M. (1993). *What we know about the role of the stepparent.* National Stepfamily Resource Center. Retrieved from http://www.stepfamilies.info/articles/the-role-of-the-stepparent.php

A research-based summary of stepfamily challenges and supported strategies to prompt effective stepparenting

Taylor, C., & Taylor, G. (n.d.). *Blended family? The 5 secrets of effective stepparenting.* Empowering Parents. Retrieved from http://www.empoweringparents.com/Blended-Family-The-5Secrets-of-Effective-Stepparenting.php#

Five ways to promote successful stepparenting

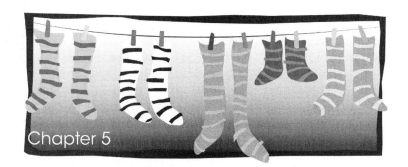

Chapter 5

Stepfather Families

The study of the role of fathers in the family has been largely relegated to the examination of the effects of the father's presence or absence in the family (Ford, Nalbone, Wetchler, & Sutton, 2008; Hofferth, Forry, & Peters, 2010); if the father is present, his role is usually that of the financial provider (Ford et al., 2008; Palkovitz & Palm, 2009). The role of the mother has traditionally been viewed as more critical to the development of the children, with fathers distanced by out-of-home careers and disparaged in terms of parental adequacy through comparison to the "maternal template" (Hill, 2011). With the rise of stay-at-home fathers, however, newer notions of fathering are replacing the provider and disciplinarian models; fathers are being represented as caring, nurturing, emotionally involved coparents, sharing domestic responsibilities and participating in family life (Genesoni & Tallandini, 2009). The study of fathers has begun to consider the complexity of the father's role beyond work–family obligations (Goodsell, Barrus, Meldrum, & Vargo, 2010), encompassing multidimensional contributions to children's well-being beyond financial support (Fogarty & Evans, 2009; Olmstead, Futris, & Pasley, 2009; Palkovitz & Palm, 2009). Now confronted with the "twin responsibilities of providing economic and emotional support for their family" (Genesoni & Tallandini, 2009, p. 315), fathering holds the potential to be dually defined between spouses. Schenck et al. (2009) identified the following roles for fathers (referred to later as the *5Ps*):

- participator/problem solver (engaged, need fulfillment for children, direct contact, availability; fostering responsibility, independence, and self-reliance),
- playmate (more high-energy physical play than moms engage in, muscle building, coordination, physical contact, dream exploration),

- principled guide (away from punishment, guidance to socially acceptable behavior, differences between right and wrong; experience and understand consequences of actions; correcting and encouraging),
- provider (still a vital role and critical societal expectation, to provide care in addition to resources), and
- preparer (for life challenges, family values, and morals; advise about educational and career goals, importance of education, of being honest and valuing work; teach children how to be parents).

The emergence of new frameworks for fathering leaves many fathers, and couples, without real-life models (Ford et al., 2008; Schenck et al., 2009). Ford et al. discussed a 2005 study that analyzed popular child rearing books and discovered that only 4.2% of the content referenced fathers, whereas 95.8% of the content focused on successful and effective mothering. These books provide an indication of societal notions of the relative value of fathering as compared to mothering. Nevertheless, data from the National Center for Fathering (2009) survey found that 89% of Americans agreed that it is important for children to live in a home with both their mother and father, 92% agreed that fathers make a unique contribution to their children's lives, and 70% agreed that the physical absence of fathers from the home is the most significant family or social problem facing America. The data confirm the importance of a father figure in the home but do not address the social reality: In many families, a stepfather is the father figure. (Chapter 8 discusses nonresidential biological fathering.)

"Fatherhood is more complex than sometimes assumed by the models family scholars use" (Goodsell et al., 2010, p. 3). Given Schenck et al.'s specification of the 5Ps of fathering, it is easy to recognize the challenges of the role beliefs facing fathers today. The prevalence of stepfamilies has given rise to the notion of the social father, which refers to a man who assumes the father role toward the children of the woman to whom he is married or with whom he is living. A purely biologically based conception of fathering is likely to have "limited utility for the fully explicating the parenting practices of biological and social fathers" (Berger, Carlson, Bzostek, & Osborne, 2008, p. 626; Hill, 2011; Parent, Saint-Jacques, Beaudry, & Robitaille, 2007). Thus, "transitions within fathering represent relatively uncharted territory" (Palkovitz & Palm, 2009, p. 3), which is especially the case for stepfathers.

Experiences of Stepfathers

The role of first-time fathers and the role of custodial fathers require drastic reevaluation and conceptualization when considering the role of the stepfather. Social institutions and the legal system offer little assistance in defining the stepfather role (Berger et al., 2008; Hofferth & Anderson, 2003; McGoldrick & Carter, 2005). Bereft of useful role models, stepfathering "prompts new ways of looking at the shifting interrelatedness of fathers' sociocultural surround" (Goodsell et al., 2010, p. 20).

Stepfathers face four types of challenges (Goldenberg & Goldenberg, 2002). The first revolves around the stepfather's status within the step-family. Berger et al. (2008) discussed the expectations of equal parenting between biological and social fathers (i.e., equal engagement, availability, and responsibility) despite the role ambiguity for the stepfather. Stepfathers serve as socializing agents and make positive contributions to the functioning. The stepfather might have difficulty positioning himself; he cannot impose a style of "fathering" on the stepfamily but may not recognize this, or he might feel ill equipped to negotiate his position with his spouse and with the children. The definition of the emotional roles that he plays is far more nebulous and uncertain. In some cases, there is ongoing tension as the stepfather strives to impose his definition on the family members, only to be repeatedly rebuffed. In other instances, the stepfather withdraws into a passive role, awaiting his wife's direction on how to be the stepfather; yet her definition of the stepfather role might say more about her needs than his need to contribute and may be based on her areas of parenting limitation than on an assessment of his parenting strength. These issues can be discussed by the couple privately, not in the presence of the children; they can talk about the strengths the stepfather can contribute and the needs of the family, so that expectations are based on capacity to provide and are openly negotiated between the couple.

The second challenge is that of space: Where does the stepfather fit, or perhaps, does he fit at all within the "parenting" picture held by each stepfamily member? In complex stepfamilies where the children of each spouse are in residence, the biological father matters more to his biological children than he does to the stepchildren. Therefore, it would be easier for him to withdraw into parenting his children only and relegate the stepchildren to the total care of their biological mother, but this approach would create a schism in the stepfamily, as though two distinct families live under one roof. Splitting parental authority in this way might be less conflict ridden than trying to integrate all household members, but this type of arrangement would probably not be what the couple hoped for when they decided to merge their households. In simple stepfamilies, where a man marries a woman with residential children, the stepfather's level of involvement with the children may vary greatly based on child age, with younger children being perhaps more receptive to his role and older children being more indifferent to him (King, 2009; White & Gilbreth, 2001). The stepfather's persistence in creating a presence may revolve around day-to-day functions, special occasions, his own hobbies and interests, and his general demeanor in his interactions with his stepchildren. This issue of "mattering" to the children is also influenced by the stepfather's enactment of his supposed authority as a parent. It must be clear that any authority enacted reflects "house" rules and mutually decided parameters, which implies the support of the mother. Such a framework of interaction prevents the children from playing their mother against their stepfather and also avoids placing the mother in a no-win position of supporting either her children or her spouse.

It has been well established that the amount of authority the stepfather attempts to exercise is negatively correlated with mattering to the stepchildren (Hofferth & Anderson, 2003; Kinniburgh-White, Cartwright, & Seymour, 2010). In other words, the more the stepfather seeks to impose his authority, especially if his authority differs from that of the biological mother, the less connected to him the stepchildren will feel. This situation becomes more confusing if the stepfather's own biological children reside in the stepfamily home and are subject to his discipline and if the stepfather cannot agree with the mother's parenting practices. A 1996 study (cited in Hofferth & Anderson, 2003) argued that stepfathers should be friendly and supportive but not try to be coparents; they have responsibility for children but little authority, apart from that given by the mother and accepted by the children. The resolution of this dilemma (i.e., the extent of the stepfather's authority) has far-reaching consequences for the stepfamily unit. Kinniburgh-White et al. determined that a maladaptive relationship with the stepfather creates a risk factor for negative child and family outcomes, while a positive stepfather–stepchild relationship is associated with good marital quality, stepfamily adjustment, and child well-being. These authors identified four themes common to adolescents' reflective narratives of effective stepfathering: (a) the children felt supported, (b) the stepfather shared family activities and treated the mother well, (c) the stepfather exhibited gentleness and strength in his relationships with all the children, and (d) the stepfather was very cautious about exerting his authority.

The fourth challenge for stepfathers is related to the stepfamily relationship evolution. While the stepfamily marriage results in an "instant" family unit, the integration of the stepfather is far more gradual. In essence, stepfathers must progressively create their own identity as a person of worth and value to the children, while balancing the parenting expectations of their wives. Each stepfather–stepchild interaction is an opportunity for the stepfather to be seen as practical and offering emotional support, without attempting to impose covert control or critical judgment (Higginbotham et al., 2012). The stepfather cannot base his effort on children's responses but rather persist in his interactions with the hope that it will result in the type of relationship with the stepchildren that he envisions. However, White and Gilbreth (2001) have found that a significant minority of stepfathers and stepchildren do not think of each other as family. With sufficient rebuffs from children, stepfathers may withdraw to the roles of chauffeur, bankroller, and handyman, which may be adequate for stepfamily maintenance but seemingly lacking in the potential emotional affiliation and confirmation that the stepfather may desire but not know how to manifest.

In summary, Gold (2010) concluded that stepfathering is more complex and less negative than initially imagined but distinctly different from biological fathering. However, "difference" simply implies what a role is not, rather than clarifying that role, emphasizing the "indistinctness of a self-created identity" (p. 210) facing stepfathers. The freedom that stepfathers enjoy to create their own identities cannot be separated from the confusion they might experience and the uncertainty of success, so the stepfather may search vainly for some guidance on assuming this new role. Stepfathers struggle in their new roles because of "unrealistic expectations. and undeveloped cultural norms" (Higginbotham et al., 2012, p. 77). Pettigrew (2013) remarked that the stepfather identity has "implications for stepfather's psychological health as well as health, well-being achievements of stepchildren" (p. 26) and must be based on self-enacted positive definitions of stepfathering as supported by the stepfamily members. Such expressions of stepfathering must reflect shared beliefs between stepfamily members about the rights and responsibilities of the stepfather. Gold (2010) asserted that this "consistency in cognitions leads to overall stepfamily adjustment" (p. 209); however, stepfathers remain confronted with both popularly held negative stereotypes and shifting versions of what it means to be a father. By exploring these stereotypes and then reauthoring them, it might be possible to create more positive stepfather scripts.

Dominant Social Myths About Stepfathers

Myth #1: The Stepfather's Job Is to Discipline the Children

The traditional role of fathers is limited to providing economic security and household authority. For men who hold such a view or for their wives who may share this vision, this is an appropriate role for the male figure in the family. The home is considered a legitimate venue for men to demonstrate their strength. Nurturance remains the primary responsibility of the mother, and the father's task is to remain "tough," "aloof," and "rule bound."

Myth #2: The Stepfather is a Friend of the Stepchildren

Recognizing the hazards of imposing the "iron rule" of the disciplinarian and the importance of winning the children to his side, the stepfather might abandon parenting completely and become an adult accomplice for the children. Siding with the children against the discipline of the mother, encouraging secrets from the mother, and advocating for the children with the mother are all attempts to "buy" the affiliations and affections of the stepchildren.

Myth #3: The Stepfather's Responsibility Is to Compensate for an Inadequate Experience With the Biological Father

Stepfathers may hold a jaundiced view of the absent father. If residual acrimony from the divorce and subsequent period of single parenting continues to contaminate the parenting relationship of the divorced couple, the new stepfather may be subjected to a litany of complaints about the nonresidential father. Some of the expressed concerns may be valid. The stepfather may hear those concerns as his wife's request or demand for reparative fathering for the children or as a counterweight to their experiences with the biological father; the stepfather might then act in ways to offset the stated deficiencies in the absent parent.

Myth #4: The Biological Father and the Stepfather Are in Competition for the Child's Love and Support

Society and the legal system encourage the belief that children have only one father at a time. Using the premise that (stepfather) proximity trumps biology and history, the stepfather seeks to develop an identity as the opposite of the stepfather and perhaps to vocalize those comparisons to convince the children of his superiority.

Myth #5: The Stepfather Expects and Should Receive Immediate Loyalty

The notion of "immediate family" carries with it the expectation of instant affiliation and receiving the stepchildren's respect. This expectation may reflect the stepfather's relationship with his own biological children or exist as a "fathering template." In either instance, the stepfather may strive to impose his authority to force himself into the ongoing mother–children relationship. In the absence of the mother, the stepfather may assume a style of parenting inconsistent with the mother's, with an expectation that his presence alone will ensure its acceptance. Any reference by the stepchildren to the mother's "way of doing things" or to the absent father's style of parenting is viewed as a statement of opposition that must be suppressed.

Narratives: Stepfathers Describe Their Lives

I've been married for three years and I still have no idea how to connect with my stepchildren. If I do something of which they disapprove, they "tattle" on me to their mother. So any values that I have about fathering count for nothing . . . I am a driver, and fixer but with no respect. I keep hoping that it will get better but I am beginning to despair.

Our coparenting is a joke. Her rules for her kids are way different than mine are for my two and so what one set gets away with, the other two get punished [for]. How do we create a family unit out of this chaos? I wish that we had sat down and hashed this all out prior to the wedding. I think it would have been easier to remain a single dad and date her.

I moved in with her encouragement to be the "man of the house." What a mistake . . . from day 1 all I heard was "you're not my real dad & you can't tell me what to do (from the 10-year-old). Now her little sister is mouthing the same things. My wife just shrugs and tells me to be patient, that it will work itself out but she does nothing to support me, but boy I hear about it if I try to "parent" in a way of which she disapproves. I am at my wits' end.

These comments capture the confusion and bewilderment that characterize the role of the stepfather. The dismaying outcome of these experiences for these stepfathers may be to question the sustainability of the current marriage and to also question their own suitability as a father figure, whatever the family constellation. However, the literature cited earlier in this chapter affirms the normalcy of these concerns, implying that the issue is not specific to the stepfather but rather a characteristic of stepfather families. Based on that approach to the stated confusion, the possible solution lies not in dissolving the stepfamily unit but in examining and then reauthoring the scripts by which the stepfather functions in that family constellation (Gold, 2010; McGoldrick & Carter, 2005; Planitz & Feeney, 2009).

Myth Reconstruction and Implications

Palkovitz and Palm (2009) claimed that "transitions within fathering represent relatively uncharted territory" (p. 3). Little seems to be known about how fathers' roles and definitions of those roles evolve over time and through differing relationships; all we know is that the road is rocky and internal conflicts are inevitable as new cognitive structures are established. McGoldrick and Carter (2011) argued that stepfathers "cannot use the roles and rules of first marriage" (p. 317). First-marriage fathering transfers poorly to the stepfamily situation, and the incomplete institutionalization of the role itself provides few guidelines for effective stepfathering. The creation of a successful stepfather identity seems to lie in the "cognitive adjustments [that] need to be made by the individual experiencing the transition" (Palkovitz & Palm, 2009, p. 5). These cognitive adjustments correspond to the reauthoring process of the stepfather myths.

Myth #1: The Stepfather's Job Is to Discipline the Children

Myth Reauthoring

The role of the stepfather as disciplinarian may be achieved over time and experience with the stepchildren or not at all. The history of the mother and biological children unavoidably relegates the stepfather to a second-tier disciplinarian. In the absence of the mother or in conjunction with mutually established "rules of the home," the stepfather can intervene in a corrective fashion. However, the idea of imposing an arbitrary code of behavior for the children will not be successful.

Implications for Effective Stepfathering

The couple should discuss stepfamily discipline privately and prior to forming the stepfamily. The couple should discuss specific appropriate behaviors, consequences, and discipline styles that both adults can accept. Then these expectations are presented as household rules to the children by the biological parent in the presence of the other parent. Children are told how the rules will be enforced, how each adult will adhere to the household's code of conduct, and that children are expected to respect the interventions of both parental figures. Discipline will be corrective, not punitive. It is more facilitative for household rules to be designated as "expected behaviors" with specific positive consequences as well as the clarification of a system of sanctions when the expected behaviors are not displayed.

Myth #2: The Stepfather Is a Friend of the Stepchildren

Myth Reauthoring

Stepfathers want to be seen as friendly. However, the children do not need an adult friend; they have several peers to fulfill that role. In addition, being a "friend" to stepchildren may imply that the stepfather will side with them against their mother, and that is not a positive role for the stepfather either as a parenting figure or as a spouse.

Implications for Effective Stepfathering

Friendliness can be expressed in two ways within the stepfamily. The first method is to become interested and invested in the children's activities. The "entry role" in this interaction is as a participant and "cheerleader," not as a coach or corrector. The children will appreciate being validated in their activities and will, over time, welcome more stepfather input. These activities can be as special as expressing a unique talent or as common as homework or as mundane as a household chore. The stepfather's course of action is to continue to offer help or assistance, rather than wait for the stepchildren to approach him. They may be reluctant to do so, because either they are not used to asking or they fear rejection, so the stepfather should take the first step. The stepfather should never see the child's rejection of assistance as a personal affront; he should continue to offer assistance so that the children remain aware of his willingness.

The stepfather can also invite the children to participate in his pasttimes or hobbies. Because the children have not grown up with him, his interests are unknown to them, and so his presence does offer an opportunity for new experiences. Even if they reject his offer, they will appreciate being asked to participate and perhaps over time will accept the invitation. Again, the stepfather should not take rejection personally, nor should he conclude that he must abandon his preferred activities to accommodate the children. The family unit must be able to accommodate conjoint and individual hobbies and leisure activities.

Myth #3: The Stepfather's Responsibility Is to Compensate for an Inadequate Experience With the Biological Father

Myth Reauthoring

The stepfather's responsibility is to augment the children's experiences with their biological father. The stepfather should respect the children's emotional bond with their biological father and attempt to offer a second experience of bonding with a male figure. The stepfather should not present himself as "better" than the biological father. If the biological father has been absent from the children's lives, the mother and stepfather need to carefully consider what he can offer that the mother cannot, what unique qualities he can bring to the children, what special interests or hobbies he can share, as the children experiment not only with what it means to have a "new father" but also with having a father at all.

Implications For Effective Stepfathering

Stepfathers must separate what they hear about the absent biological father as a spouse and as a father. The divorce may have sundered the emotional bond between spouses, but it does nothing to sever the emotional bond between father and children. In the majority of cases, absent fathers desire an ongoing relationship with their children, and the stepfather must honor and support that relationship. The stepfather should never discuss with the children his perceptions of their biological father; the children might very well be secretly afraid that their new stepfather might attempt to separate them from their father. Although the biological father and stepfather may never bond, they must agree to collaborate in terms of providing ongoing consistent positive male presences in the lives of the children.

Myth #4: The Biological Father and the Stepfather Are in Competition for the Child's Love and Support

Myth Reauthoring

Stepfathers must honor children's feelings of affiliation to their biological father and demonstrate that there is room in their lives for two "fathers" who will work collaboratively. Stepfathers should show that they respect the primacy of the biological father in the life of the children and support their ongoing relationship with him. Stepfathers must also strive to distinguish between the roles of the children's biological father: his ongoing role as father and his past role as spouse to the children's mother.

Implications for Effective Stepfathering

Children possess sufficient affection and need for affiliation that they can accommodate two father figures. After all, grandfathers do not compete for the connections with their grandchildren, and each grandfather holds a unique place in their hearts and offers distinctive experiences to each child. Perhaps this model is generalizable for the stepfather and biological father. The relationship between the biological father and his child predates the stepfamily, and any attempt to discourage, diminish, or destroy that relationship will have only negative repercussions for the stepfather. The stepfather need not worry that the children's connection to the biological father in any way impedes their capacity to connect with him. In fact, honoring that connection will contribute to the stepchildren's feelings of affection for the stepfather.

Myth #5: The Stepfather Expects and Should Receive Immediate Loyalty

Myth Reauthoring

The stepfather must recognize that, as with any new adult presence in the family, there is going to be a "testing" period, the length of which depends partially on the stepfather's patience and consistency and also on the continued invitation to the stepchildren to participate with him on a variety of experiences. The myth could be rephrased as follows: The stepfather will strive over time to earn the children's loyalty.

Implications for Effective Stepfathering

Gold (2010) advised stepfathers to allow time to develop a workable relationship with each stepchild; the process and length of time is determined by the age and gender of each child. Stepfathers are encouraged to let the children set the pace for the relationship in terms of emotional closeness and shared activity. They are also directed to honor the stepfather role by insisting on the 4 "R's": respect, roles, responsibility, and realistic expectations.

Adamsons, O'Brien, and Pasley (2007) compared biological and stepfathers of first graders to see how contextual factors influenced child rearing practices. The study was driven by the increase in stepfamily households as identified in census figures (although the authors suspect that the figures may underestimate the actual number of such families by 1/3) and by the research on father involvement and quality of engagement with children, as compared to simple presence in the household. The authors hypothesized that while stepfathers and biological fathers share equal tasks, stepfathers are less engaged and emotionally close to stepchildren than are biological fathers. For the purposes of this study, father involvement in child rearing was determined by the division of work and the father's perceptions of contribution to child-related household tasks; *quality of engagement* was defined as the observed quality of interaction, focusing on sensitivity, responsiveness, supportiveness, and stimulation of cognitive development. The results of this study showed that there were no differences between the groups of fathers in their involvement in child rearing and, surprisingly, that there was also no difference in the quality of interactions with the children. They also found that stepfathers tend to hold less traditional beliefs about parenting than do biological fathers. The researchers concluded that in stepfamilies as compared to nuclear families, there is a much stronger correlation between the quality of the marriage and parental involvement. In fact, the stepfather–stepchild relationship might be a key variable in maintaining the marital relationship. Such studies offer only "snapshot" pictures of stepfamily dynamics, and the authors expressed the need for longitudinal data to trace family dynamics over time.

In summary, reauthoring the social myths related to stepfathers eliminates competition with the absent biological father and places a realistic time frame for relationship development. Stepfather patience, consistency, and realistic expectations are strong foundations for the evolution of the stepfather–stepchild relationship.

Issues of Cultural Diversity and Stepfathers

The professional literature on stepfather families in the cultural groups of interest here includes no published studies at all on Hispanic stepfathers. I hope that readers of this book will monitor the literature and perhaps uncover sources specific to that group of stepfathers that did not exist when this book was written. (Needless to say, lesbian stepfamilies, a cultural group of interest to this book, are excluded from consideration in stepfather families.) This section will discuss what is known about African American and gay stepfather families.

In African American stepfamilies, there seems to be no reported differences with the biological father in terms of identity and involvement with children (Forehand, Parent, Golub, & Reid, 2014; Stewart, 2007). Both father figures seem to offer similar accessibility to the children, direct interaction, play, outings, and responsibility. There does seem to exist a covert mandate for stepfather: They must "pay to stay" either in terms of ongoing monetary support or participation in household responsibilities. Mothers seem to be adamant that the stepfather must contribute to the family constellation; they do not accept his mere presence as another dependent in the household. African American stepfathers may integrate more easily in the family because of a cultural pattern of accepting fictive kin, and yet their standing and authority might be less than that of Caucasian stepfathers because of the greater relative power of African American women. In comparison to Caucasian stepfathers, African American stepfathers are seen as less stressed, because less is expected of them in terms of contribution to the family system and longevity. Statistically, there seems to be an increase in cohabiting partners in African American families (Forehand et al., 2014). Socially, there appear to be negative perceptions and institutional barriers to African American men who assume the parenting roles of stepfathers, especially if they are not formally married to the mother. In essence, their role seems diminished because the sustainability of the current relationship is unknown and the matriarchal hierarchy is strong.

For gay stepfathers, stepfamily life presents structural and psychological challenges not experienced in any other stepfamily constellation (Jenkins, 2013; Stewart, 2007). If the stepfather role is underrecognized by social institutions such as the legal system and church, the role of the gay stepfather is even more undervalidated. This lack of societal approval leaves gay stepfamilies with few, if any, positive images of the stepfather role, which leads to confusion for the gay stepfather and diminished respect socially. In many states, the divorce decree from the heterosexual marriage stipulates that when children visit their biological father for an overnight stay, the father's male partner, as a nonrelative, cannot spend the night in the house. If the children's mother blames the gay partner for the dissolution of her marriage, fear of legal retaliation is pronounced; gay stepfamilies live with the threat that new custody or visitation court battles could further reduce their access to the children. At present, the gay stepfather has to deal with the artificial division of two families under one roof: The two gay partners form a family unit, but during visitation, the family consists of the biological parent and the children; the gay partner is not part of the picture. There is also a common concern that the children will not accept the father's sexual orientation and blame the gay stepfather for the dissolution of the marriage. Finally, gay stepfathers make the same mistakes that heterosexual stepfathers make; they are susceptible to the same myths about their roles, discussed earlier in the chapter.

Conclusion

The roles of stepfathers are not always clear, and no sound models are available for reference, an unsettling situation for the stepfathers and the professionals who work with stepfamilies. The absence of guidelines creates an opportunity for the positive definition of the stepfather role, free from social hindrance and precedence, in a way that will serve stepfathers, children, and the stepfamily as a whole. Defining a role on the basis of "values that honor relational ties based on affection and moral responsibility, rather than biology alone" (Gold, 2010, p. 213) would appear to be the challenge facing stepfathers today.

Resources

Anonymous. (n.d.). *Stepfathering adolescents: It takes patience, flexibility and humor*. Family Relations. Retrieved from http://www.fathers.com/s5-your-situation/c21-step-dad/stepfathering-adolescents-it-takes-patience-flexibility-humor-2/

Straightforward relational tips for stepfathers

Diane. (2010). *The challenging role of stepdad*. Today's Modern Family. Retrieved from http://www.todaysmodernfamily.com/index.php/3156

The struggles of stepfathers and five directions for successful stepfathering

Pasley, K. (1994). *Reflections on men's lives following divorce and remarriage*. National Stepfamily Resource Center. Retrieved from http://www.step-families.info/articles/mens-lives-following-divorce-and-remarriage.php

The challenges faced by divorcing and remarrying men

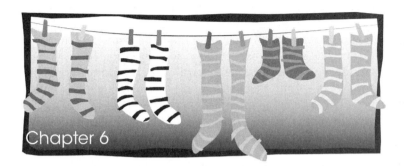

Chapter 6

Stepmother Families

Stepmother families are, by far, only a minority of residential stepfamily constellations—a surprising fact given that most of the myths and fables pertaining to stepfamilies relate specifically to the stepmother family. Goldenberg and Goldenberg (2002) estimated that stepmother families make up only about 16% of the total stepfamily population; this is because fathers are rarely awarded sole custody of the children, and joint custody arrangements in cases of divorce are uncommon (Gosselin, 2010). As a result, stepfamilies consisting of a man, his biological children living in the home, and his wife (stepmother of the children) are less frequently encountered than families consisting of a man who is stepfather to his wife's residential children and has nonresidential children of his own.

Historically, stepfamilies have been formed when men remarry because they have children at home whose biological mother died; they remarry to replace the "mother" role in the family. That role became the defining aspect of the second wife and distinguished the two "mothering" roles. Greeks and Romans used multiple terms to distinguish the "replacement mother" from the biological mother. The term *step* originates from the word *stoep*, or bereavement, reflecting a time when stepfamilies formed after the death of the mother; the term first appeared in use in 1400 or so. A stepmother was chosen for her capacity to raise the children with little help from the father (Dainton, 1993). She was seen as a "second-best" or "replacement" mother.

Perceptions of stepmothers are less favorable than perceptions of biological mothers (Doodson, 2014). Myths regarding stepmothers proliferate around the world and include elements of jealousy, incest, or greed. Dainton (1993, citing Smith, 1953) identified 345 versions of the Cinderella story worldwide, demonstrating that the evil stepmother is a global archetype. The stepmother is always responsible for improper behavior; the stepchildren are seen as victims who usually rise above the inherent wickedness of their stepmother (Anonymous, 2006).

With such widespread stereotypes of stepmothers, it is safe to assume that little girls do not grow up wanting to be stepmothers (Anonymous, 2006). In stepmother families, the rules, boundaries, and expectations of first-marriage parents do not apply (Carter & McGoldrick, 2005b). Goldenberg and Goldenberg (2000) attributed the increased stress in stepmother families to higher societal expectations for parenting from women than men. As evidence of this pressure, Gonzalez (2012) conducted an informal chat-room poll of stepmothers and found that respondents described the experience of being a stepmother as "scary" (74%) and "hard" (78%).

Experiences of Stepmothers

Today, stepmother families are more likely to be formed as a result of divorce rather than the death of the mother. Regardless of the causes of divorce, fathers retain a marriage bias (Goldenberg & Goldenberg, 2002); they tend to remarry and divorce with high expectations of each subsequent union. In some sense, stepfamilies are like arranged marriages: The children from prior marriages and the stepparent may be barely acquainted, yet everyone is expected to live together in the intimacy of one home (Anonymous, 2006). In the traditional arranged marriage, partners may barely have met prior to the marriage, but in the stepfamily it is the stepmother and the children who are unfamiliar to one another (Doodson, 2014). In a traditional marriage, the couple usually have time alone before the addition of children, while the stepmother family enjoys no such coupling hiatus: Simultaneously with the marriage come the instant addition of children plus the presence of their mother (formerly the husband's spouse). Moreover, while traditionally males fulfilling a father role might not be involved in the family dynamics except perhaps in issues of finance and discipline, mothers, including stepmothers, are expected to become more involved in the family dynamics and to base a sense of relational worth on the success of those relationships and on the satisfaction of each family member. This social expectation is hard for biological mothers to meet; the task becomes nearly impossible when the new mother has little prior history or affiliation with the children and may seem in relational competition with the nonresidential biological mother for the affections of the children.

By nature, and regardless of the personalities involved, stepfamilies are characterized by built-in structural ambiguities, loyalty conflicts, guilt, and membership problems (Carter & McGoldrick, 2011; Doodson, 2014). Although the stepfamily appears for all intents and purposes to be a nuclear family, it differs in critical ways: the uncertainty of the role of the stepmother, the preexisting allegiances between children and biological mother, possible tensions between the husband and ex-wife, and concerns about the adequacy of the enactment of the stepmother role. In addition, stepmothering seems imbued with a number of intrapsychic issues and interpersonal relational tensions that interact and sustain one another.

64

Among the stepmother's intrapsychic concerns, Goldenberg and Goldenberg (2002) raised four areas of stepmother role ambiguity: membership (who are the "real" members of the family?); space (where do I belong? what space is mine?); authority (who is in charge of discipline, of money, of decisions?); and time (who gets how much of my time, and how much do I get of theirs?). The stepmother's confusion on these issues is likely to be shared by all stepfamily members (Gosselin, 2010). The stepmother is likely to feel exploited by household labor and child care and by societal expectations to be self-sacrificing and completely devoted to children not of her choosing (Stewart, 2007). Spring (2010; see also Doodson, 2014) discussed the insecure attachment bonds in all stepmother family relationships (expressed through anxiety, anger, ambivalence, and withdrawal), which leads to feelings of isolation, exacerbated by feelings of abandonment by the husband/father in the stepmother role. Repeated conflict and ongoing tension result in a growing hopelessness and a fear about the futility of resolution. Stepmothers may feel abandoned when the partner sides with his children, and the children's rejection and disregard lead to feelings that one is an "outsider," welcomed and supported by no one in the stepfamily.

The stepmother's interpersonal stresses arise in relation to her husband and biological father of the stepchildren, the stepchildren, and the nonresidential biological mother (Doodson, 2014). These interpersonal dynamics are strongly influenced by the residence of the children and the visitation protocols (Craig & Johnson, 2010; McGoldrick & Carter, 2011; Stewart, 2007). The residence of the children is a crucial factor. If the children reside with the biological mother, the stepmother will find it harder, if not impossible, to connect with the children in any sort of parental role (Stewart, 2007). The visits feel disruptive and exploitive, with the stepmother reduced to either a "servant" role or amusement provider. It may be difficult for her to watch her husband try to parent nonresidential children: She has less or no input regarding visitation schedules or discipline, which may cause marital strain and generate conflict with the biological mother. Stepmothers tend to assume responsibility for family relationships and, if the relationships are unsuccessful, they often strive more frantically or intrusively to "direct" the step relationships in desirable directions. This usually results in the frustration and exasperation of the stepmother, the animosity and resentment of the children, the anger of the biological mother, and tensions within the marital relationship.

Stepmothers assume responsibility for the day-to-day running of the house and nurturing the children. If the husband is ineffectual and the children are unhappy, the stepmother might try to "parent" the children, which may not be supported by the father and may be begrudged by the children. This "remedial parenting" is tricky: If she assigns chores and disciplines her own children, she is seen as a good parent, but if she does this with stepchildren in the parenting absence of the children's father, she is seen as cruel. The children complain to their father about the stepmother, and the marital relationship may begin to crumble. In addition, there may be ongoing issues of jealousy over the time and resources spent on his children, either at the expense of the needs of her children or the marriage, and by the spouse's ongoing coparenting relationship with the noncustodial mother (Anonymous, 2006; Spring, 2010).

In terms of interpersonal dynamics between the stepmother and stepchildren, it is unrealistic to expect her to love stepchildren as she does her own; they lack a shared history and a common affiliation, and the biological mother is part of the picture, even if she is not physically present. Initially, at least, stepchildren are not in a position to like anyone: They may be hurt and upset by the dissolution of the old marriage and the imposition of the new stepmother; attempt to monopolize the father's time and resources; jealously guard the memory of their mother; and generally feel insecure and unhappy about their futures.

Spring (2010) explained the dynamic as follows: The children feel disempowered by the new stepmother, whom they view as their father's new priority, and the stepmother feels marginalized by the children. With her self-esteem based on parental and family roles, repeated rejections by the stepchildren lead to cycles of insecurity and guilt, expressed through more intrusion and more rejection. Socially, stepmothers take the brunt of the blame for stepfamily turmoil. They are expected to supply all the needs of the children with no voice in the running of the household—in other words, they have responsibility without authority (Spring, 2010). The stepmother may be jealous of the children's mother (Stewart, 2007) because she has a history with the stepmother's new husband and especially so if she lives in a home chosen and decorated by his ex-wife. In addition, the stepmother may feel exasperated by the failures and frustration of her numerous affinity-seeking strategies with the stepchildren; by comparison, the biological mother holds the child's complete adoration without seeming to try (Anonymous, 2006).

Lambert (2010) reviewed the assessments of adult stepchildren and identified five categories of stepmother relationships:

1. Negative ("My stepmom and I only get along because we have to. I don't like her.")
2. Negative-neutral ("Because she is married to my father, and out of respect for him, I show her love even though it is a false love.")
3. Neutral ("She married my dad.")
4. Positive-neutral ("She married my dad and because she is a female figure, I can go to her at certain times when I need someone.")
5. Positive ("She is genuinely nice. She makes my father smile. She has never treated me any different from her own children.")

Carter and McGoldrick (2005b) reported that stepmothers experience more stress, less satisfaction, and more symptoms than stepfathers. Shapiro and Stewart (2011) described the negative mental health consequences of adopting a stepmother role, including more depressive symptoms. Katz's (2010) study found stepmothers to be depressed and exhausted from doing all the relational work; they endure incessant phone calls, interruptions, and accusations from the ex-spouse and unsympathetic attitudes from friends.

Given the strains implicit in these experiences, the role of the stepmother elicited more negative comments than those reported concerning any other family member. Stepmothers are seen as less affectionate, good, fair, kind, loving, happy, and likable and more cruel, hateful, unfair, and unloving. Stepmothers must contend with two sets of polarizing and contradictory expectations: They are evil and cruel, and they must compensate for the absence of the biological mother by being loving and competent. This paradox obstructs the establishment of a consistent stepmother identity (self-concept of beliefs about who she is and how she ought to be perceived and treated in social life). Usually, the creation of an identity assumes choice, but the stepmother role is thrust upon a woman married to a man with children. The resulting issues and dynamics then are not personality bound but label bound.

The stepmother believes that she is judged on these beliefs in both public and private life; she is supposed to love the children as if she is the parent but is prevented in law and fact from being a parent. The myths maintaining this difficulty show no signs of abating (Dainton, 1993).

Dominant Social Myths About Stepmothers

Myth #1: Stepmothers Should Compensate for the Absent Mother

Given the absence of the mother either through her demise or noncustodial status, stepmothers need to "fill that gap" and become the "super-parent" for the children. Stepmothers are responsible for meeting all the emotional needs of the children, and their success depends on resolving whatever difficulties the children have confronted prior to the stepfamily. In addition, stepmothers must also recompense the children for any relational shortcomings on the part of the biological mother and yet, while doing so, never speak critically of her.

Myth #2: Stepmothers Will Become the Children's Mother

As an extension of Myth #1, it is expected that the stepmother will earn the title of "mother" and do so instantly. If not forthcoming from the children, she must work more diligently to earn that moniker.

Myth #3: Stepmothers Should Insist on the Husband Prioritizing the Couple Over His Children

The stepmother chose her husband, who happens to have children. If the children do not reside with the stepmother, there is no reason for their father to cater to them when they visit or live with the couple, nor should he cater to his ex-spouse.

Myth #4: Stepmothers Who Don't Love Their Stepchildren Are Unreasonable, and so Are Children Who Don't Love Their Stepmothers

Given the nature of the mothering role, and the assumptions of an innate maternal instinct, the stepmother and stepchildren should feel an instant bond to each other. This love must be unconditional, immediate, and reciprocal. The absence of this affection indicates the eventual dissolution of the stepfamily unless somehow this ideal relationship can somehow be fostered. Moreover, the stepmother is responsible for its strength and sustainability, even if the children do not reside in her home.

Myth #5: The Stepchildren's Mother and Any Relationship With Her Should Be Avoided

The biological mother's absence from the children's lives either on a full-time or part-time basis indicates her unsuitability to be their parent; the husband's perceptions of her as a parent must be accurate. She does not mean well for the children, the new marriage, or the stepfamily and ought to be avoided; when possible, the children should be protected from her. Therefore, it is the stepmother's responsibility to conduct all family business with the absent mother and to shield the children from her influence.

Narratives: Stepmothers Describe Their Lives

I don't know any little girls who dream of becoming stepmothers. I have regrets of my past but I still look forward to the future as hopefully as I can muster. Being a stepmom for over 5 years has been both a thankless and awesome experience. At first, I never thought that the title had really much to do with my identity, but being an outsider to the dynamics of a broken home—these happenings directly impact me, my lifestyle and the future of my own biological children. I was and *still am* a foreigner to my family's household and history. It's a conflict: being too involved, not caring enough, stepping in where I shouldn't, and yet needed to always be accessible; you are wicked no matter what. (Nov., 2013)

I was never sure I wanted kids. In my twenties, on days that I thought I did want kids, certainly this thought followed: "Yeah, but not until after my husband and I have had years of just us two, seen and experienced the world, accomplished our goals, and bonded as a couple." Now I'm in my thirties and there doesn't seem to be time for that. I can imagine being alone and adopting a child when I'm 40 because maybe ten years seems like enough time for me to live the life I've been wanting and come into my own. It makes me wonder what level of sorrow I may experience over not carrying my own child, but I think I could come to terms with that.

To complicate these thoughts, I think I met the love of my life. He's definitely head and shoulders above anyone I've ever been with in over a decade of dating. He really seems like my perfect match. The ways we fit together exceed anything I ever imagined. The wrench in the whole relationship is that he has three kids from a previous marriage, and he has them full-time. . . .

I want to preface everything I'm about to write down by saying I love his kids, and I feel completely selfish for having these thoughts. I've been wishing there would be a magical shift in my mindset, but so far it hasn't happened. It's only a few months into this relationship so hopefully I just need time. My boyfriend and I became serious pretty quickly because we were amazed at how well we fit together. We want to get married. If he didn't have the kids, I'd be 100 percent certain about our future. Instead, sometimes I think about being alone.

We haven't been able to date in the way to which I'm accustomed. I need kid-free alone time with him, and he's made that happen to the best of his ability. I enjoy our alone time, I feel it's absolutely necessary, yet I still feel guilty for inconveniencing his family. It didn't help when this past weekend his stepmom asked when I was planning to "move in and start helping with the kids." My man doesn't share her feelings, he's patient with me and listens to all of my fears. Still, I feel pressured, even from myself. I believe these kids need me. And I'm just not ready. Not by a long shot.

It would help if perhaps they were better disciplined. Don't get me wrong, they are good kids. They are 6, 5, and 3 years old. They are loving and cuddly and curious. They tell me they love me, sometimes they call me mom. I want to be there for them like they deserve. Their father lets them get away with a lot, he says because he has guilt over what they went through when their mom left. There's a lot of getting what they want when they want it, and a lack of consequences. I have ideas for how I want things to change when I move in, I've discussed these ideas with their father and he's very receptive; the problem is that I know he won't implement anything until I'm there to crack the whip. This creates the added pressure that makes me feel so overwhelmed. I don't want him to think I'm saying he's a bad dad or that his kids are brats. I don't think either of those things are true. He knows how I feel but I'm not beating it into the ground. However, this is the central point of why I'm overwhelmed and questioning our relationship along with the path my life should take. (Dec., 2013)

I have been with this man for 4 years and we just got married in June. His son every time we get him makes sure I am out of the picture. He lies and tells his mom how nasty I am to him when his dad is not around which is untrue and many people have witnessed how he talks to me and treats me. I feel like getting a divorce because of this boy. It is heart breaking to know that the man I love so much, I just think I can't spend my life with him if his son carries on like this. (Jan., 2014)

These comments reveal common hopes and realities of stepmothers; the initial category characterized by feelings of optimism and anticipation and the latter category characterized by feelings of resignation and regret. Anonymous (2006) insisted that it is time to change the image associated with stepmothers, to replace the old fairy tales with more positive images.

Myth Reconstruction and Implications

Dainton (1993) encouraged clinicians to assist individuals to "overcome myths and misconceptions about this family role" (p. 97). Katz (2011) argued that media innuendo and tacit stepmother myths do much to damage stepmother families. Societal misconceptions of the stepmother role are perpetuated by the media; it is time to separate the person of the stepmother from the unrealistic and oppressive myths under which she and her stepfamily members must attempt to function. The following sections offer examples of reauthored stepmother myths to foster more positive stepmother functioning and perhaps offer a greater probability for the success and sustainability of stepmother families.

Myth #1: Stepmothers Should Compensate for the Absent Mother

Myth Reauthoring

Stepmothers provide a new experience of "being mothered" to the children. This experience is based on a particular woman's mothering strengths and is intended to augment but never replace the children's original experiences of being mothered by the nonresidential mother. Children have ample room in their hearts and lives for many loving figures; adults need never be concerned about competing for a child's affection.

Implications for Effective Stepmothering

Stepmothers should begin their new roles as they intend to live them. From Day One, they should insist on courtesy and respect. It's hard to generate a positive relationship if these dynamics don't happen at the beginning of a relationship with children and other family members. Therefore, the stepmother has the opportunity to define her own stepmothering role unique from that of the biological mother. Doing so emphasizes to the children and to the biological mother that there is no intent to replace, just to supplement, the experience of mothering the stepchildren. The stepmother should not allow anyone else, including her husband, to define her role or expectations. Because he is the biological parent in the home, it is his responsibility to lead in all areas of parenting and for the stepmother to contribute to the parenting expectations and to enact those conjointly created and explained to the children.

Myth #2: Stepmothers Will Become the Children's Mother

Myth Reauthoring

Stepmothers have no desire to replace the memories and experiences of biological mothers. The stepmothers revere those memories as foundational for the children. The stepmothers wish only to augment those histories with more current and positive experiences of being mutually respected, nurtured, and supported.

Implications for Effective Stepmothering

Stepmothers are not and will never expect to be viewed as the children's mother. Stepmothers do not seek to occupy a role that belongs to the biological mother in her day-to-day interactions with her children or in the memories of the children (in the event that the biological mother is not involved in their lives). The stepmother affirms the ongoing connection between the children and their biological mother and seeks to offset any perceptions of competition with the biological mother. Furthermore, the stepmother honors the primacy of that emotional link as a way to prevent any sense of jealousy or expectations of divided loyalties among the children. It is critical for the stepmother to see that any perceived negativity from the children is usually directed toward the role being enacted by the new person, and not the person herself, so she should try to not take these negative feelings personally. These negative feelings would be projected upon anyone who took the absent mother's place, but children should be assured that a stepmother plays a different role although she may have some "mothering" responsibilities. Stepmothers are encouraged to enjoy the time with stepchildren based on shared interests and activities, absolved of the primary parenting responsibilities.

Myth #3: Stepmothers Should Insist on the Husband Prioritizing the Couple Over His Children

Myth Reauthoring

Stepmothers understand the priority of the children, especially when that relationship with the father is limited to visitation rather than residence. Children hold history and memory with the father, and his role is contingent on their continued closeness. Supporting these visits does not diminish the marriage nor threaten its sustainability.

Implications for Effective Stepmothering

Stepmothers will always share their husbands with his children for the rest of their married life. A strong bond may exist between a husband and his children, and attempts to interfere with this attachment will be resented by both the father and children. However, it is the father's responsibility to balance attention to both his parental and marital relationships. Jealousy can be avoided if stepmothers realize and accept this dynamic early in the relationship. However, while the father must balance the roles of fathering, either full-time or part-time, the stepmother can hold the marriage as her priority and regard the stepmothering as a secondary function. If the couple doesn't work on their marriage, nothing the stepmother does will work. A united front—the husband and wife—must coincide with stepmothering as relationships are to be built with the rest of the family. When a couple supports and loves one another, they can function at the most favorable levels to help the rest of the stepfamily members.

It is helpful if the stepmother is prepared when she enters the marriage and stepfamily. First, the stepmother must recognize the distinctions between first-marriage and stepfamily couples and between family life and parenting functions. Given the rejection of the first-marriage template for the stepfamily, the stepmother can learn about what is and is not "realistic" for stepfamily life. Third, the stepmother can gather information about her new family members before the marriage, which can help her negotiate relationships, understand family dynamics, and anticipate (and hopefully prevent) significant obstacles to stepfamily success.

Myth #4: Stepmothers Who Don't Love Their Stepchildren Are Unreasonable, and so Are Children Who Don't Love Their Stepmothers

Myth Reauthoring

It is unreasonable to expect a child to feel instant affiliation to any new adult, be that adult a teacher, coach, or stepmother, no matter how loving, caring, attentive, and supportive that adult figure may be. Those feelings may never emerge for a variety of reasons having nothing to do with the qualities of the stepmother. Trying to force or falsify such feelings detract from the reality of whatever relationship is being developed.

Implications for Effective Stepmothering

There are no ideal role models for stepmothering, which can be seen as a blessing and a curse. The absence of stepmother role models means that there are no rules or preset expectations to which one must conform; however, each stepmother is left without guidance to figure out how to do this "right" or "well." If there are no guidelines for stepmother success, one could make the case that social myths offer guidelines only for stepmother failure. Therefore, the responsibility or opportunity for success rests with each stepmother, who must decide what will work best for her.

The stepmother role should be based on what is comfortable for the stepmother, the children, and the family as a whole. The father's love for his wife does not obligate his children to love their stepmother. The children may not bond instantly with the stepmother, and the reverse is also true. Stepmothers need not feel guilty if they don't immediately feel love and affection for their stepchildren. It takes time to build relationships. Family members should treat each other with respect and fairness, remembering that it is possible to be caring and nurturing, even if there are not great feelings of mutual love. However, the stepmother may take proactive measures; investments of love in stepchildren far outreach returns. While perhaps dreaming of and working toward a closer relationship with the stepchildren, the stepmother should feel reassured by and accept a relationship with each child that is "good enough."

Myth #5: The Stepchildren's Mother and Any Relationship With Her Should be Avoided

Myth Reauthoring

The biological mother can provide a rich source of information about the children to the stepmother. In addition, demonstrating to the children that both mothers intend to collaborate provides the children with a sense of stability and continuity (Gonzalez, 2012). The endorsement of the biological mother for the stepmother role will prove valuable in building a respectful and caring relationship with the children.

Implications for Effective Stepmothering

To develop a good working relationship with the biological mother, the stepmother should try to make clear that she separates the reports of her husband about his ex-wife and the experiences of the children about their mother. Stepmothers can benefit from talking to and sharing with the other mother. The two mothers don't have to like one another, but it is helpful if they can work together for the welfare of the children. Not only can the biological mother offer insights into the children's history and unique personalities, but the evolution of continuous expectations between households can also make the transitions of the children easier.

Issues of Cultural Diversity and Stepmothering

Little is known about the effect of culture on stepmothering. A literature search using scholarly engines and popular search engines did not yield a single article pertaining to Hispanic stepmothers and very little information regarding African American and lesbian stepmothers. This dearth of information may be an indication that stepmothers are so miniscule a group that their presence is overlooked. In addition, the U.S. Census Bureau does not consider stepfamily households as a "family unit" if the children reside less than 50% of the time in the stepfamily home and the stepmother is the noncustodial parent. Cohabiting couples do not qualify as a family (or stepfamily) unit. All these factors may contribute to the challenge of recognizing stepmother families and, other than perhaps volunteer sampling or web-based blogs, complicate their accessibility and scholarly study.

Relevant studies about stepmothers contain too few responses from African American stepmothers to analyze (Stewart, 2007). Most African American women see the role as difficult and undesirable, and single African American women under 35 seem less willing to marry men with children. Some comments suggest that disciplining stepchildren is less of a concern to African American stepmothers, perhaps because African American children are more accustomed to being disciplined by "other mothers," such as adult relatives, neighbors, and fictive kin. African American stepmothers tend to make fewer distinctions between biological and stepchildren, assuming care of all of them as a group; they also rely on religious and church affiliations for support with handling family stress.

Lesbian stepmothers hold the same romantic ideals and commit the same mistakes as heterosexual stepmothers (Stewart, 2007). There is a unique challenge around shared parenting in that traditional hierarchical ideals (roles of mothers as distinct yet complementary to roles of fathers) hamper coparenting. Because gender cannot determine role enactments, how are such distinctions made? It becomes expedient for all roles to be recognized and then assumed based on parenting strength and preference, with openness to learning and assuming new roles as needed. A second challenge exists if the sexual nature of the couple relationship is kept hidden from the children. Akin to the issues within gay-stepfather families, there may be a tension between wishing to be open with the children about the lesbian relationship yet fearing the children's rejection if they do. The single consistent finding is that stepmothers can discipline only in the absence of the biological mother and then only along preestablished parameters.

Insufficient information on the dynamics of stepmother families is available for the cultural groups addressed in this book. One hopes that researchers and social scientists rise to the challenge of contacting these stepmothers and learning more about their experiences, crucial ground-work for advancing appropriate conceptualizations and interventions to promote stepfamily success.

Conclusion

Dainton (1993) advocated that stepfamily members "must combat the firmly entrenched myths of the wicked stepmother and instant love" (p. 97). It is the mutual acceptance of these myths by stepmothers and stepchildren that present challenges (Lambert, 2010). Communication is key; yet for stepmothers, what is communicated is the preexisting, and largely unconscious, perspectives on the role of stepmother. The agenda then for stepfamily members is to reauthor these stories based on actual stepmother–stepchild experiences and then author new, more realistic and more positive expectations of stepmothering. Until this is done, identity issues will remain salient for stepmothers for some time to come.

Resources

Hoffman, R. M. (1995). *Why is stepmothering more difficult than stepfathering?* National Stepfamily Resource Center. Retrieved from http://www. stepfamilies.info/articles/why-is-stepmothering-more-difficult-than-stepfathering.php

Differing social expectations for stepmothers and stepfathers

Potter, K. F. (1994). *What's a stepmother?* National Stepfamily Resource Center. Retrieved from http://www.stepfamilies.info/articles/whats-a-stepmother.php

A conversational piece between two children describing a stepmother

Visher, E. (1994). *Fantasy expectations of life as a stepmother.* National Stepfamily Resource Center. Retrieved from http://www.stepfamilies.info/articles/fantasy-expectations-of-life-as-a-stepmother.php

Unrealistic stepmother myths

Chapter 7

Mutual-Child Stepfamilies

More often than not, the trajectory of family life includes the postmarital addition of children. For first-married couples, this addition comes after the couple establishes a stable identity as a couple. When children are part of the marriage, however, members must simultaneously establish both an identity as a married couple and a family identity. For stepfamilies, the act of having mutual children is not inevitable. As Deal (2010, echoing Ganong & Coleman, 1988) observed, stepfamily couples ponder whether to "have a baby together" (p. 687) whereas first-marriage couples might instead discuss the timing of the pregnancy. This suggests that the decision to add a mutual child to the stepfamily is thoughtfully made.

No precise data on the number of children born in remarriages are available (Bernstein, 1997; Ganong & Coleman, 1988; Stewart, 2005a, 2007) because this information is not collected in national demographic surveys. Stewart (2005a) claimed that one half of all remarried women have children in remarriage and that about one third of all women's childbearing occurs in second marriage, meaning that approximately one third of stepchildren have a stepsibling (Stewart, 2007). An estimated 1.3 million stepfamilies include a mutual child. At what point in stepfamily life is the addition of a mutual child optimal? How might the new child contribute to the solidification of the stepfamily and the marriage, and how might the new child be accepted within the stepfamily? These are some of the questions that stepfamily couples ask themselves. The child born into a stepfamily is unique because he or she is related to everyone in the stepfamily even though not everyone may feel related to one another (Stewart, 2007). Even the adjectives used to describe this child (*shared, mutual, joint, ours*; Stewart, 2007) indicate that the child occupies a role that is anything but ordinary. Deal (2010) reviewed the literature and found no consensus on the advisability of adding a mutual child to the stepfamily, a process that requires a "reorganization of family life and parental responsibilities" (Stewart, 2005b, p. 461).

Experiences of Mutual-Child Stepfamilies

Deal and Petherbridge (2009) referred to the topic of having a mutual child as an "under-studied aspect of stepfamily life" (p. 242). Little is known about the long-term impact of the mutual child on the child, marriage, stepsiblings, or sustainability of the stepfamily unit, but there does seem to be a consensus regarding the optimum stage of stepfamily development in which addition of the mutual child seems more conducive to individual, marital, and family functioning. Papernow's 1993 model of stepfamily evolution, which identifies three distinct stages in a stepfamily's evolution, is cited by researchers in this area (e.g., Bernstein, 1997; Deal, 2010; Kela, 2009; Stewart, 2005b, 2007).

In the *early stage*, parents and stepparents try to create an instant family, to heal with love a family that had been pulled apart. Children, however, hang on to their fantasies that their biological parents will get back together again. This suggests two differing versions of the stepfamily: The adults see it as a permanent system, and the children hope that it is a temporary interlude. The adults are making an effort to establish a new identity and create dynamics, whereas the children want the dissolution of the new stepfamily and a return to either their nuclear family or the family they had with one biological parent. In the early stage of stepfamily life, the challenge is to balance the needs of the existing children within the direction chosen by the adults. This stage is characterized by experimentation, oscillating patterns of closeness and distance with stepparent and stepsibling and the tenuous evolution of a stepfamily identity and sustainability.

In the *middle stage*, the adults and the children have worked through whatever uncertainty they had that the stepfamily unit would persist, and an integration of sorts has been achieved but one that is based on assimilation rather than on negotiation of diverse needs and desires. This stage is when the stepfamily members begin to present more clearly their dreams for the new family unit, and it can be a tumultuous time for the family. The stepparent mobilizes to bring about changes that lead to inclusion and recognition of his or her authority. When these changes are negotiated successfully, the couple are true partners, and each has a relationship with each child that does not require intervention by the other adult. An estimated 5 to 7 years is required for stepfamilies to reach this stage. Paradoxically, this is also the stage in which one or both adults feel that the stepfamily is not viable and consider its termination. If the adults do not feel secure in their roles or do not see a future for the stepfamily, then clearly the addition of a new child would only exacerbate the tensions and upend relational priorities within the stepfamily.

During the *established remarriage* stage, intimacy and authenticity in stepfamily relationships have been achieved. Both stepparent and stepchild feel like insiders, and the solidity of the couple provides a strong center to the stepfamily. After ensuring that all current members feel secure and established within the stepfamily, the criteria for possible inclusion of a new member seem addressed. These authors opined that it is better to wait until the stepfamily has ripened before having a mutual child.

However, not all couples want to wait 5 or more years before stepfamily relationships have settled into an easy intimacy. An unplanned pregnancy might occur; sometimes the woman's age makes it advisable not to postpone pregnancy; and sometimes the parents want to narrow the age gap between children in the stepfamily. These factors may encourage the couple to shoulder the added emotional work of having a child earlier than the optimal timing suggested by Papernow's model. It may not be possible to wait to realize the four conditions that contribute to an easier transition to the addition of the mutual child: stable and positive stepfamily relationships, positive relationships between children and their biological parents and stepparents, children residing with the stepfamily, and young age of children.

The anecdotal literature (Bernstein, 1997; Deal, 2010; Stewart, 2007) regarding the receptiveness of stepchildren to a sibling offers some tentative insights. The parents hope that the stepchildren will be as happy and excited as they are, but there is usually some jealousy inherent in bringing any new child into a family, and bringing one into a stepfamily is no different. Children can be excited yet worried about how much time a new baby will require and how much attention will be taken away from them, and they may fear being replaced. They may express fear of losing a parent to the new child.

Children's responses to a new child in the family may vary based on sibling position within the stepfamily. The acceptance of a sibling is usually easiest on the older children. The status of the firstborn is not threatened by the arrival of the new child. However, older teens may wonder about the impact of a new baby on family finances and resources for what they want and the intrusions into personal space. Therefore, the older children may be seen as siblings or perhaps even aunts or uncles if the age difference is large.

Children between ages 6 and 10 seem to have a hard time with the presence of the new baby. Preteens oscillate between accusing the parents of "unfair" treatment and nurturing and taking care of the new child themselves. A new baby gives them an opportunity to demonstrate how "mature" and "responsible" they can be and to engage in activities that are younger than their chronological age but made legitimate by the baby.

The addition of a new baby to the family is usually hardest on the youngest child and on the only child. It is usually hard for younger children to watch a parent fall in love with a newborn and find them so cute and adorable. All of a sudden, the youngest in the family looks so much "older" and seems more difficult, and the new baby gets all the love and attention. The role of "youngest child" or "baby" has been usurped, and the displaced child may feel lost or confused about the resulting family position. This role change becomes even more complex if the child is still the youngest when he or she lives apart from the stepfamily (e.g., while living with the other biological parent's new family). This shift becomes harder too if the new baby and displaced child are of the same gender. Sometimes the child may compete for parental attention by regressing in behaviors and "out-baby" the new child.

The child born in a stepfamily—the only child in the house who has two biological parents living together—carries an unusual burden. Born into a family where there may be tensions and factions, the couple hopes that the mutual child (the "one that is ours") will bind fragments of two families. Usually acutely attuned to that peacekeeping mission, the mutual child also often feels very special, holding a good sense of his own worth. The bonds can be particularly strong when the mother is a first-time mother who has had to struggle to win over her stepchildren. Half siblings left on the periphery of this passionate embrace, though, may end up resenting the mutual child. The mutual child is thus faced with a mixed bag of privilege and hostility.

The impact of the mutual child on the marriage seems mixed. In choosing to bond with another adult, having another child may be the one thing farthest from the mind of a single parent, yet the very presence of children throughout a couple's courtship makes the issue a hard one to ignore. As two people become more intimate, and their lives become more and more entwined, the relationship between the children and potential partner becomes an important variable for many adults to consider when deciding to commit to the relationship. Partners who have no children of their own and may have no expressed desire to have any may begin to wonder, after continued proximity to children and responsibility for their care, what it would be like to be a biological parent with the new partner. Many factors encourage this, including the romantic notion that having a child together is a way to express love and commitment to the new spouse and the belief that this would provide an opportunity to "do it (parenting) right," to have children lucky enough to live with both parents and to complete the family-building process. However, these (positive) motivations are often coupled with a fear of stepfamily failure (which carries with it two sets of visitations and child support payments), the current ages of the spouses as being too old to begin child rearing, the financial constraints especially if child support is being paid, and the sense that one has "enough" children to raise.

Consider a stepfamily consisting of a biological father and stepmother who have no children together. The prospect of having a child together might make the man worry that his children might get jealous; along with the usual fears and anxieties of having a child, he might be anxious about bringing a baby into a stepfamily, and he might be less motivated, because he has already experienced having children and he might worry about being caught between the new baby and his own children. He may feel guilty, especially if his first children show behavioral signs that they are not enthused. The prospect of becoming a mother, especially if the woman enters the marriage with no children of her own, is likely to be more joyful for her than it is for her partner.

Research findings, though rather limited (Deal, 2010; Deal & Pether-bridge, 2009; Ganong & Coleman, 1988), seem to consistently show that the decision to have a child in a stepfamily serves a protective function for marriage but results in lower marital satisfaction. This birth does not cement the bonds of remarriage emotionally but legally does bolster the commitments between the parents. As is the case in nuclear families, having a child diminishes marital satisfaction initially, but then it is rebuilt over time. Remarried couples will make the right decision only after considering the many changes an "ours" child will bring to all members of an evolving stepfamily. When feelings about having a child together differ, the spouse who places the survival of the couple above the outcome of the decision about a mutual child generally finds a way to make peace with a partner's greater need.

The challenge of "blending" two families has been discussed throughout this book. Effectively coparenting one's own children and one's spouse's children involves a complex dynamic. If conflict and tension-filled step-parenting have a detrimental effect on the sustainability of the stepfamily, as has been demonstrated in this book, one wonders about the impact of a third "category" of child on stepfamily cohesion. In the words of Downs (2003), the addition of the mutual child is "important to the construction of stepfamily identity yet little understood" (p. 36).

Downs (2003), Deal and Petherbridge (2009), and Fletcher (2010) seemed to agree that the new birth may raise questions of parental loyalty, especially among nonresidential stepchildren. Who will the parent love more, the biological children who reside elsewhere or the new child who lives in the stepfamily home? The new child does add a sense of family identity as he or she is the only child in the stepfamily who might share a surname with both parents. In addition to solidifying the couple's structural commitment to the relationship, the new child brings role certainty and role clarity—it is simpler to be a parent than a stepparent.

Ganong and Coleman (1988) found that having a mutual child "is no more likely to strengthen emotional bonds in the stepfamily as it is to disrupt them" (p. 695). Stereotypes about the role of the mutual child might set the stage for stepfamily tension and disappointment.

Dominant Social Myths About Mutual-Child Stepfamilies

Myth #1: The New Child Will "Cement" the Stepfamily

Social narratives equate child bearing with the definitive stage of family formation and evolution from a couple dyad to a family unit; the addition of a child defines the legitimacy of the family unit as distinct from and perhaps as the more mature evolution of the couple unit. With those no-tions in mind, it would seem socially imperative that the new stepfamily couple add a mutual child, regardless of the number of children that each spouse brings to the family from previous relationships. Moreover, the mutual child serves a function that the stepchildren cannot, which is to unite the adults in an equal coparenting role.

Myth #2: It Is Critical to Have This Mutual Child Early in the Stepfamily Life

In families in which the adults cohabited prior to the marriage, there is a sense of urgency to bear children, and this is true of both first-married couples and couples forming a stepfamily. Having "established" the couple unit, the next step, popularly conceived, is to add children to the family unit. This step may be viewed as the spouses' commitment to each, to the family unit, and to a future together. There may also be external pressure by grandparents and peers.

Myth #3: The New Child Will Be Loved and Accepted by All the Other Children

The notion that children will automatically love their new baby siblings may be more wishful thinking that actual observation. Even in nuclear families, the addition of children displaces the other children from their family roles and generates a sense of disequilibrium until new role-based identities are established. Expectations for a baby boy may differ from those for a baby girl born into a family with an older male child. The introduction of each new child "upsets" the standing social order and demands that the siblings' functions, rights, and responsibilities be refigured. The new child also demands parental love, attention, and resources, which may provoke feelings of jealousy for the new child. Therefore, siblings' "love" for a new child emerges over time as the parents balance the needs of all the children; the children feel accepted and confirmed in their new places within the family as precursors to the enjoyment, acceptance, and fascination with the new brother or sister.

Myth #4: The Parents Will Be Equally Excited by the Mutual Child

The notion of parental urges runs deep in our societal unconscious. The potential for joy and anticipation on the part of the parents-to-be seem an expression of societal narratives around the pending birth. Moreover, each parent must share the joy and excitement of the other and any trepidation can be easily explained as to-be-expected "cold feet," which will instantly dissipate upon seeing one's new child for the first time. In addition, and unique to the stepfamily, this excitement ought be present regardless of the number of previous children one has, and regardless of the feelings of one's biological children toward the new child.

Myth #5: The Presence of the Mutual Child Will Mirror That of a Child in a First Marriage

Given the relative absence of understanding of stepfamilies in general, and of those stepfamilies with a mutual child, the model used to understand the impact of the new child on the stepfamily is that of a nuclear family.

In that system, there is a period of adjustment as existing siblings, grandparents, aunts, uncles, and extended family assimilate the new child while maintaining existing relational dynamics. However, one guarantee in this situation is that, after the period of adjustment, the new child will be fully accepted by all family members.

Narratives: Stepfamily Members With a Mutual Child Describe Their Lives

> I wanted to have a child of my own with my husband. Being just a stepmother was not satisfying enough. In fact, being a stepmother was anti-satisfying.
>
> —Web-based comment (February, 2014)

> Part of me feels pressure of having a child because I am getting older and part of me doesn't want to create any more stress in our lives than we already have.
>
> —Web-based comment (January, 2014)

> In my opinion, the benefits of having my own children versus only having stepchildren are far-reaching; stepchildren were a big disappointment to me. But biological kids are a heart-fulfilling, life-altering experience. As a stepmother I feel like a bad parent and a constant failure. As a biological parent, I don't have to share my kids with another woman, I feel like a success. The contrasts are extreme. Each day I fail as a stepmother and succeed as a mom.
>
> —Web-based comment (March, 2014)

> The cracks in our family began to show as my baby became real to me. I found myself less tolerant of my stepchildren. The power of my emotional response floored me. But when a new baby is welcomed into a home where at least one parent has children from a previous relationship, stepfamily dynamics are split wide open again. (Fletcher, 2010).

It is noteworthy that these quotes are from stepmothers, not fathers of a mutual child; one can only speculate about the reasons for that. The comments suggest the schism that may arise between the mother and two categories of children and hints at the possible rift that might be created for the biological father of the stepchildren and the mutual child. One thing is certain: These comments do emphasize the weight of the impact of the addition of the mutual child to the stepfamily and the need for a more balanced cognitive schema through which to anticipate and respond to the addition of the mutual child.

Myth Reconstruction and Implications

Myth #1: The New Child Will "Cement" the Stepfamily

Myth Reauthoring

It is unfair to place the responsibility for family cohesion on a baby, whether the child is born in a nuclear family or a stepfamily. The responsibility for family cohesion, integrating stability, and security with opportunity for change and development rests solely with the parents, regardless of the family constellation.

Implications for Effective Stepfamily Functioning

What does seem clear is that the arrival of the new child will generate "relational" ripples through multiple-home stepfamily system (Deal & Petherbridge, 2009). The type of ripple is based in the strength of family cohesion as created by the parents. In families with too much structure and stability, there is little room for accommodation for the needs of new family members, and those members are directed to adapt to the family. In those families with excessive flexibility and spontaneity, the family may become wholly organized around the mutual child, placing him or her in too central a place and role in the family and expecting all other roles and relationships to become of secondary importance.

The parents need to determine how to maintain the existing relational roles plus integrate additional roles (that of new parent and perhaps of new stepsibling). The relational issues needing resolution may include how will the family stay the same when the new child arrives (what will change), how will the marriage remain the same (and what will change), and what losses (and joys) can each family member expect to experience.

Myth #2: It Is Critical to Have This Mutual Child Early in the Stepfamily Life

Myth Reauthoring

Having a mutual child in the stepfamily needs to be based not on timing but rather on the stability of the stepfamily relationships. It is critical to ensure that the stepfamily members have settled satisfactorily into their new roles prior to expanding those roles with the addition of the new child.

Implications for Effective Stepfamily Functioning

The developmental framework proposed by Papernow (1993) and cited earlier in this chapter is useful to keep in mind when considering ways to enact the reauthored myth. Rather than measuring time in the stepfamily that has elapsed as the critical variable in the timing of the pregnancy, the couple in a stepfamily would do well to focus on relational task accomplishment. The operative question can be reframed as, "Are the stepfamily and its members ready to add the new child?" This readiness is then evaluated by the status of the marital relationship, the development of effective stepparenting relationships with all children, the resolution of divorce issues with ex-spouses, and the anticipation of how the addition of the new child will affect all stepfamily members.

Myth #3: The New Child Will Be Loved and Accepted by All the Other Children

Myth Reauthoring

Each child added to any family constellation provokes a range of emotional responses in the present children and generates a transition that takes time, patience, and nurturance to resolve. In addition, and specific to the variability in stepfamily constellations, the residency of the children will contribute significantly to this process of adaptation. Resident stepchildren will tend to acclimate, perhaps with greater reactivity and immediacy to the new child, but will move through this reworking more rapidly than will stepchildren who reside elsewhere and only visit the stepfamily and mutual child and whose visits seem to present a new stepfamily upon every visit.

Implications for Effective Stepfamily Functioning

Deal and Petherbridge (2009) offered five considerations for supporting the stepchildren, be they residential or visiting, through this time of change. These authors recommended lengthy conversations with all children and extended family about how life will change after the baby is born. The new child has an independent identity but also displaces the youngest child in the family hierarchy, elevating that child, perhaps unwittingly, to the status of "older" or "middle" child with the responsibilities, roles, and rights unanticipated. This change happens whether or not the stepchildren live with the new child.

To foster stability in the children's lives, parents should keep the half-siblings' lifestyle, visitation, and parental contact unchanged. There may need to be separate time dedicated to each of the existing children to reinforce the parent's continued affiliation and affection. While it may be easier to interact with the children separately, parents are also encouraged to orchestrate frequent contact between half-siblings to encourage bonding. Allowing the children to get to know their new baby sibling, free from parental direction, will facilitate a more natural bond and will result in more direct lines of connection from the stepsiblings, whether in residence or not, with their new sibling. Part of the stability revolves around raising all of the children with similar values. Children in stepfamilies may already feel confused if the custodial parents and noncustodial parents hold differing values and expectations, but those discrepancies can be assigned to households and accommodated accordingly. The level of confusion grows when intrafamilial differences in values and expectations are present. One can only imagine the family chaos if two parents each hold their own biological children to differing standards and have differing standards for the stepchildren plus a third set of expectations for the mutual child. Stability is enhanced when all the children in the same household are held to the same expectations, as relative to age, gender, and family position.

Parents should refrain from being defensive or offended if stepchildren voice frustration over how the new baby has affected them. These frustrations are based on what they perceive as "losses" in their lives. Those feelings need to be legitimized and addressed by the parents in the home. In addition, what the child gains by the presence of the new child might help balance the child's sense of displacement and disgruntlement.

Myth #4: The Parents Will Be Equally Excited by the Mutual Child

Myth Reauthoring

It may be overly optimistic to assume that spouses share equal feelings at exactly the same time about any life event. This assertion may be less applicable in situations where both spouses are experiencing a life event for the first time and, so, for each spouse the event is a novel experience; neither has any past history on which to rely or which might influence one's emotional responses to the new event. However in the stepfamily unit, at least one spouse has experienced the birth of a new child prior to this event. Thus, one must expect that each spouse will have differing emotional responses to the addition of the new child.

Implications for Effective Stepfamily Functioning

Couples should explore individual expectations about the addition of a mutual child and how parenting responsibilities will be shared (Deal & Petherbridge, 2009). The expectations will be based on whether each spouse has children who make up part of the stepfamily and whether the anticipated mutual child marks a spouse's first experience as a biological parent. The spouse with biological children might be concerned about balancing the duality of parenting in a way that honors the ongoing commitment to one's existing biological children yet welcomes the new addition to the stepfamily. This challenge might apply to both spouses in the stepfamily if that constellation includes children from two prior relationships.

For the spouse who is becoming a biological parent for the first time, there is also the need for balance one's deep feelings of love and commitment for the child and one's ongoing role as a stepparent. In such a situation, the novelty of the birth is unique to only one partner while its occasion may reawaken memories of the births and experiences with young children that one's current spouse cannot share. What is required is a sense of transparency on the part of the spouses, honesty of communication, and legitimization of differing affective responses to this event—*differing* meaning only the recognition of individual histories coinciding around this experience.

Myth #5: The Presence of the Mutual Child Will Mirror That of a Child in a First Marriage

Myth Reauthoring

To reauthor this societal belief, it is critical for the stepfamily adults to acknowledge the motivation behind the addition of the mutual child. Children cannot be reasonably expected to fulfill a relational expectation (such as family identity or cohesion) at which the adults have yet to succeed or have failed. Moreover, given the disparities between the developmental needs and tasks of first marriage as compared to stepfamilies, the new child in a stepfamily cannot be expected to affect the system nearly as much as in a first marriage, simply because the two family systems are so different.

84

Implications for Effective Stepfamily Functioning

The responsibility for the health or dysfunction within a family unit must be assumed by those with the most maturity, insight, knowledge, and skill to effect positive change. Accepting that assumption, the parents must accept this trial. While issues such as establishing and nurturing a healthy family identity and sense of cohesion are perhaps more arduous in the stepfamily than in a first marriage, expecting children to provide these functions places the children in an untenable position. Given the qualities described in this section as necessary for success in these endeavors, children, regardless of age, maturity, or willingness, are ill equipped to fulfill these expectations. Therefore, parents should carefully assess the motivations and expectations held regarding the new child.

In many ways, adults in stepfamilies are at a loss as there is a dearth of information about the impact of mutual children on stepfamily dynamics. However, reliance on what is known about the impact of children in first marriages can provide no more than a foundation around which parents can discuss what they expect or hope might result from the birth of a mutual child; they must then temper those notions with an understanding of stepfamily dynamics and life. The need to tailor-make these ideals as a reflection of the realities of stepfamily life empowers the adults to develop a collaborative perspective that is based in lived stepfamily experience and can be enacted within that stepfamily by the parents.

Issues of Cultural Diversity and Mutual-Child Stepfamilies

In researching and writing this text, I have been exasperated to find very little published research on topics related to stepfamilies—not in the professional literature and not on general web sources, either. None of the sources that offered resources were of help. My search of professional and popular databases such as PsycINFO and Google Scholar using combinations of the terms *mutual child*, *our child*, *shared child*, or *joint child* with the four groups of interest (African American, Hispanic, gay, and lesbian stepfamilies) yielded no results.

As a result, clinicians must approach these stepfamilies with expressions of awareness and cultural sensitivity. Introduction of the literature presented in earlier sections of this chapter may resound with these stepfamily members or may be rebutted in favor of lived experience. Researchers and counselors alike can approach this topic from any perspective unhampered by previous findings and consider whether what is known about majority stepfamily functioning with a mutual child does indeed fit these other constellations.

Conclusion

In 1988, Ganong and Coleman noted the complexity of the functioning of mutual child stepfamilies and suggested that both longitudinal studies to trace family functioning over time and multi-member qualitative studies might provide the understanding and direction of efficacious clinical service. This decision to add a mutual child however is not uniform across stepfamily constellations. More than 20 years later, Deal and Petherbridge (2009) echoed those same opinions. While insufficient data has been gleaned within the interval between the two publications, what remains clear is that "stepfamilies merit investigations designed to explore the motivations and decisions that affect their lives and to answer questions that could improve the quality of those lives" (Ganong & Coleman, 1988, p. 697).

Resources

Amato, P. R. (n.d.). *Living in a stepfamily: The child's view*. National Stepfamily Resource Center. Retrieved from http://www.stepfamilies.info/articles/living-in-a-stepfamily-the-childs-view.php

Research studies of children's perceptions of stepfamily life

Anonymous. (n.d.). *Biological children & step children—Can the bond be equal?* The Labor of Love. Retrieved from http://www.thelaboroflove.com/articles/biological-children-step-children-can-the

The differing affective connections between parents/stepparents, biological, step and mutual children

Deal, R. L. (2003). *Getting remarried with children: Effective pre-stepfamily counseling*. Smart Stepfamilies. Retrieved from http://www.smartstepfamilies.com/view/prestepfamily-counseling

The struggles and successful strategies for stepfamily life with children

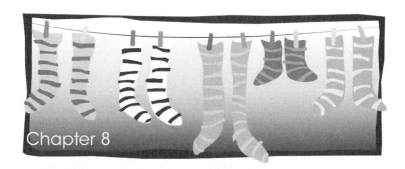

Chapter 8

Extended Stepfamily Constellations: Relationships With Ex-Spouses

As the number of stepfamilies grows, so too does the number of noncustodial parents. According to Hofferth et al. (2010), about 25% of all children (48% of African American children, 16% of White children, and 13% of Hispanic children) do not live with their biological fathers; about 16% do not live with their biological mothers.

Legal statutes continue to maintain that "American society constrains children to two or fewer parents" (Gunnoe & Hetherington, 2004, p. 561). Yet growing numbers of children are living in stepfamilies and may have perhaps four active parenting adults: the biological parent and stepparent who reside with them, an absent or noncustodial biological parent, and in the cases of complex stepfamilies, the noncustodial parent of the children's stepsiblings. This gap between the legally sanctioned and the real-life experiences of stepfamilies contributes to the ambiguity and uncertainty implicit in relations between the stepfamily and the noncustodial parents (Erera & Baum, 2009; Gold & Adeyemi, 2013; Olmstead et al., 2009; Schrodt, 2011; Shafer, Jensen, Pace, & Larson, 2013). Both the California and New Jersey courts are beginning to acknowledge the possibility of a third legal parent; it then behooves counselors and their clients to be current on the legal statutes in the state in which they reside. This matter becomes more complicated when divorced parents reside in separate states with differing statutes. The court system can finalize issues of custody, visitation, and financial support between divorcing spouses, but it cannot prepare the divorcing adults for the trials of coparenting with an ex-spouse .

Skogrand, Davis, and Higginbotham (2011) recognized the importance of this multifaceted relationship for stepfamily adjustment (i.e., coparenting with an ex-spouse) and satisfaction and advocated for a "normative-adaptive perspective" (p. 69) in this relationship. The normative-adaptive orientation assumes a period of transition through uncharted, unfamiliar, and undefined relational processes. The enacted (as compared to the legally mandated) practices of coparenting require skills of negotiation and compromise to achieve parental consistency and harmony despite separate residences. This resolution is based on two conditions: the cessation of the spousal divisions that prompted the divorce and a desire to work together to remain effective, yet separate, parents.

Shafer et al. (2013) concluded that "ties to an ex-spouse whether based in past problems or current interpersonal dynamics, add complexity to postdivorce relationships and can stress such unions" (p. 630). Schrodt (2011) identified this relationship of coparenting between ex-spouses as one of the most defining aspects of this family constellation and predictive of stepfamily sustainability. Issues of trust, fairness, and good faith seem tied to effective postdivorce functioning in both the stepfamily and between the stepfamily and nonresidential biological parent. In addition, content-focused issues of parental authority, role performance, and legitimacy as coparent in the stepfamily; changes in contact time or closeness with children; and reestablishing trust in the ex-spouse's parenting ability all color the postdivorce renegotiation of parental role, power, and boundaries (Martin-Uzzi & Duval-Tsioles, 2013).

Martin-Uzzi and Duval-Tsioles (2013) claimed that without knowing "the ex-spousal system," one could not have "a complete picture of the couple's experience" (p. 44). This statement attests to both the ongoing relational presence of ex-spouses within the stepfamily and the importance of understanding how these relational systems function.

Experiences of Ex-Spouses

Stewart (2007) maintained that the focus on remarriage tends to ignore any consideration of the former spousal–parental system: "both stepparents and biological parents seem unaware of, or are in denial about, the difficulties that may lie ahead" (p. 54). Gold (2010) too concluded that "much of the research on stepfamilies ignores interactions with nonresidential parents" (p. 210). As a result, little research is available on the role of the nonresidential parent. It seems likely, however, that a close relationship between ex-spouses who are trying to coparent effectively may also threaten their new marriages.

Given current child custody arrangements, nonresidential fathers constitute a greater percentage of this group (84%) than do noncustodial mothers (16%). Mothers are generally considered by courts to be the preferred residential parent, but they may relinquish their rights because of dysfunction or their inability or lack of desire to parent. (This is further discussed in the section on noncustodial mothers.)

Some nonresidential mothers and fathers wish to have no contact with their children, or are legally prohibited from such contact, but the majority continue to visit and fulfill their legal obligations and their emotional commitments. Children with involved nonresidential parents gain by the additional financial support, and the emotional support is correlated with higher school engagement among children. Consistent and high levels of visitation (communication, closeness, and authoritative parenting) are predictive of children's personal and social well-being, of collaboration with mother on school engagement, and of the socioemotional health of both the mother and children (Hofferth et al., 2010; Olmstead et al., 2009).

Some degree of conflict and hostility between ex-spouses is to be expected. According to Stewart (2007), children of divorced parents are exposed to more adult conflict than children living with their biological parents, with a greater potential for children being emotionally pulled between the ex-spouses and "forced" to choose the parent they love more. This triangulation, which usually reflects power struggles that remain from the marriage, can generate tension and anxiety as each interaction between ex-spouses degenerates into endless blaming, recrimination, and withdrawal, with the children trapped in the middle. Even anticipated contact with the ex-spouse may foster a "major source of stress and preoccupation" (Stewart, 2007, p. 127). This contact may be legally allowed so that the divorced couple can bring closure to the emotional wounds from the dissolved marriage. This lingering animosity must be settled or at least not allowed to interfere with the emerging coparenting relationship. The optimum arrangement would entail collaborative parenting (each household governed by similar expectations for the children with a consistent reward and sanction system) versus parallel parenting (each parent enacts that role in an individually chosen style, without consideration for the parenting by the other parent). In addition, any residual sense of spousal connection must be resolved as each spouse enters into new romantic relationships, or notions of jealousy or envy may interfere with the ex-spouse's new relationship and may contaminate the coparental arrangements (Gunnoe & Hetherington, 2004).

Nonresidential Fathers

As stated previously, 84% of nonresidential parents are men, and so the bulk of research has been focused on this group (Stewart, 2007). In addition, the issue of custody is related to visitation and child support, and so social agencies such as the family court system and child welfare agencies may attend to the responses and behaviors of the nonresidential father. However, this monitoring tends to emphasize the degree of compliance with court-mandated activities, not the lived experiences of these men. For this group of men, the life changes are immense and the emerging emotions powerful.

Erera and Baum (2009) discussed the critical impact of the result of the divorce and custody/visitation decisions, which replace self-defined roles of "fathering" with those imposed by legal jurisdiction (see also Gold & Adeyemi, 2013). Olmstead et al. (2009) discussed the continued role of provider through the delivery of child support. Nonresidential fathers are also hampered by a lack of practical authority on day-to-day decisions regarding the children, as a function of either their knowledge of the issue or the immediacy of a decision, which does not allow for consultation with the mother (Gold & Adeyemi, 2013). In that regard, nonresidential fathers are always playing "catch up" on the details of their children's lives (Hofferth et al., 2010). Noncustodial fathers often bemoan the artificiality of visitation, where they find themselves reluctant to discipline for fear of tainting the visit or causing the child to reject future visits (Gold, 2010; Gold & Adeyemi, 2013; Olmstead et al., 2009). Thus, noncustodial fathers find themselves unaware of the child's changing life experiences and relegated to the role of "entertainment provider" for those brief periods of visitation. Neither condition seems acceptable, but it isn't often clear how to facilitate a more "fatherly" experience.

The emotional responses of nonresidential fathers can be divided into two categories. One cluster revolves around the noncustodial father's relationship with his ex-wife concerning generic parenting disagreements (Erera & Baum, 2009), feelings of inadequacy as a parent, difficulty separating the roles of current yet absent father and ex-husband, and feelings of powerlessness and despair at not having a larger role in the child's life. The second cluster revolves around relationships with the legal system, through which the father lost his rights to children with no recourse, and a perception of powerlessness in relation to family courts that seem to favor mothers over fathers. Olmstead et al. (2009) observed that noncustodial fathers have animosity associated with child support and a concurrent disappointment with the lack of appreciation and recognition from ex-spouses and children. As a function of these massive life changes and imposed characterization of one's role as a father, nonresidential fathers struggle to build a cooperative coparenting relationship with the ex-spouse and to feel valued and important in the lives of their children (Hofferth et al., 2010). Despite these challenges, 66% of children report having good relationships with their absent fathers, described as a function of affective bonding between father and children rather than any instrumental skills (White & Gilbreth, 2001).

Nonresidential Mothers

Noncustodial mothers have diverse interactions with the stepfamily unit. Some of these dynamics are related to the noncustodial status of the mother (whether that status was her decision, instigated by the children's father, or imposed by the courts). Deal and Petherbridge (2009) referred to the noncustodial mother as the "ex-wife-in-law" (p. 155), in recognition of the reality of her presence; her children will try to keep her as an active presence in their lives, regardless of the personal feelings of their father and stepmother.

Five types of noncustodial mothers have been identified.

- The "open mom" loves the children, is collaborative in parenting, has resolved the divorce issues, and sees the stepmother as a positive force for both her ex-husband and the children. This mother tends to be one who recognized her own need to leave the marriage and wants the best for all concerned. She tends to parent from within her own parental strengths and limitations and seems dedicated to moving forward with her life and encouraging all others to do the same.

- The "me mom" tends to have left the marriage for her own personal or professional advancement, feeling constrained by the role of mother and wife. There is less satisfaction in the postdivorce relationship, because this mother tends to analyze the worthiness of the stepmother to be with her children and, by implication, qualities of her ex-husband who would choose such a woman as a stepmother. However, she tries to shield children from disruptive outcomes of conflict and change associated with divorce and her role as a mother.

- The "over-involved mom" may have been divorced because the ex-husband wanted to marry the current stepmother. There may be a residual anger toward the ex-husband for "replacing" her. Moreover, this mother seems enmeshed with her children. Her total identity centers on her need to be the center of the children's emotional lives. This insistence leaves little room for either the father or the new stepmother. Her doggedness is expressed through continual communication with the children and a lack of trust in the father's ability to parent effectively. The stepmother is viewed as competition, and any sign of affiliation or compliment on the part of the children is seen as disloyalty. All interactions deteriorate into a "me versus them" struggle, with the affections of the children used as pawns.

- The "stonewalling mom" carries continual anger and resentment toward the husband for the divorce and, by implication, toward the stepmother for taking her place. Every issue or discussion no matter how trivial becomes imbued with this residual bitterness. Coupling a no-win conflict management style with a refusal to communicate or collaborate, this mother ensures ongoing conflict, anxiety, and tension between the households.

- The distant, abusive, destructive, or addicted mother connects with children from her own selfish needs. She needs to be seen as a "good mother" even while her actions belie that description. Her individual issues render her irresponsible, undependable, and a threat to the stability of the stepfamily home, but she has no insight into her behavior. Vacillating closeness and distance in relation to the children, their loyalty will keep them pining for her affiliation and connection. Unfortunately, these promises will go constantly unrealized. The most impactful mother may be the one labeled as "destructive." This individual is dangerously angry, resentful, and bitter about the loss of custody of the children (and perhaps of the divorce as well). She has no desire to work with the stepfamily unit but rather seeks revenge; she is not deterred by legal restraints. Neither the father nor stepmother are safe from her attempts to sabotage their personal, professional, and family lives; should the children be harmed in the process, she would view this as unfortunate but not as an impediment to her actions.

The goal of intervention (should any be attempted) is to encourage the noncustodial mother to participate fully in moving forward with her own life and supporting the new stepfamily unit to do the same.

Dominant Social Myths About Stepfamilies and Ex-Spouses

Dominant social myths about stepfamilies and ex-spouses are predicated on anticipations of negativity and triangulation; getting to the point where mutual appreciation and respect are possible might be challenging. Sharing an intimate relationship with someone other than the current spouse can be awkward for everyone. Frequently, conflicts among the adults are not resolved but rather ensnare other family members, especially the children, into ongoing acrimonious and divisive arguments about every aspect of parenting and every aspect of the stepparent's relationship with the children. Social myths are built around these conflictual relationships.

Myth #1: Children Can Be Loyal Only to the Biological Parent, Not to the Stepparent

The biological parent holding this belief may overtly or covertly pass this belief system to the children. This idea of loyalty is based on fear about the possible loss of their relationship. Could it be that the stepparent will build a stronger relationship with the child than the biological parent? Is the relationship between the child and biological parent so vulnerable that it can be replaced by the stepparent? Certainly the biological parent's state of mind would have an impact. If the child knows that loyalty is a primary concern for the biological parent, this may affect the way the child treats the stepparent.

Myth #2: Divorced Couples Cannot Agree on Anything

The marital relationship ended because of conflict (and, more than likely, unresolved conflict), so the root of this myth is not hard to trace. The ex-spouses are prone to carry their history into the new relationship with the resultant complementary behaviors. The ongoing conflict is likely to affect their ability to coparent. There would be fertile ground for disagreements concerning parenting practices; the adults may not discipline the child, and the child may take advantage of this situation.

Myth #3: Divorced Couples Want the Ex-Spouse Out of the Children's Lives

In an effort to simplify the complexity inherent in stepfamilies, the residential parent may be prone to exclude the nonresidential parent from the children's lives. This is more likely if the "new family" includes two sets of children. The nonresidential parent may be insecure about the new arrangement following the divorce and feel that he or she is not able to spend "enough" time with the child.

Myth #4: The Stepparent Is Trying to "Replace" the Biological Parent

The ultimate fear is that one is being replaced. The parent who believes the third myth is most likely to believe that he or she is being replaced. The biological parent believes that it is impossible to retain a secure relationship with the child if the child has a relationship with the stepparent. This belief may be especially strong if the stepparent has a financial advantage and is able to inundate the child with gifts. By merely asserting a role in the "new family," the stepparent may be threatening to the nonresidential parent. These feelings are likely to be exacerbated if the new marriage results in a relocation that is a significant distance from the nonresidential parent.

Myth #5: All the Ex-Spouse Wants Is Financial Support

The nonresidential parent may be insecure and skeptical about the residential parent's motives; he or she may not be realistic about the costs involved in raising children or may not agree on certain expenditures (e.g., private school).

Narratives: Spouses Describe the Relationships With Ex-Spouses as Part of Stepfamily Life

I just had no idea that his former wife would be so involved in our lives. My husband is afraid of what she might tell the children so he allows her to dictate our schedule. I feel like his former wife is the other woman in our marriage.

Jenny described the big shift in the divorced family dynamic which occurred this last Christmas. Jenny is now living with a man and this was to be their first Christmas together. However it's also the first Christmas where her ex-husband was not invited to come on Christmas morning to open gifts with his and Jenny's children. Even when they were separated, he was included for the children's sake. Jenny felt it was too awkward this first Christmas with her new partner and suggested her children open gifts at her house, then go to their father's house to open gifts a second time. The surprise came when the kids returned and said they had invited their father over later for Christmas dinner. Jenny asked her new man how he felt about it. He hesitated, laughed and then generously said it was okay if it would make the kids happy. So in the end a compromise was made which took into account everyone's feelings, though Jenny said she felt awkward at the meal and was glad when it was all over.

While Steve was waiting for his kids at their mom's house for his weekend with them, his ex-wife came out and indicated that she was getting remarried. "You will really like Tim," she said, "and the kids seem to like him too. I think he will make a great stepfather for them." Steve was not too sure he liked any part of the idea. It was weird enough to be thinking of his ex-wife married to another guy. But what troubled him even more was the idea that there would be a new father figure in the life of his kids. He didn't like the thought of having another man in competition with him for the affection of his children.

I will soon be a non-custodial Mother, by choice. We are choosing to have as little disruption as possible to the kids, and by doing things this way, they will be able to remain in the only home and school they have ever known. We have a beautiful home, and thanks to the economy, this home is now worth $32,000 less than what we paid for it 10 years ago. There are houses on our street that have been on the market for almost 2 years. We would lose our shirts even if we did manage to sell, which is highly unlikely. My husband makes a very nice living. I did not go to college and have been a stay at home Mom for 9 years, so my earning potential is weak compared to his. There is no way I could stay here. With what he would need to pay me in support and to keep this house afloat, he would have nothing left to get himself even a halfway decent place. I will be buying a townhome in the area with money from the divorce settlement. The kids will be with me almost as much as they are with him. This was an extremely hard decision, but I feel that it is best for the kids. They have a great relationship with both of us. But, I am just waiting for the criticism and the dirty looks once I tell people.

To my son: I hope you understand when you're older. Why your dad has maybe grown colder. You're so young, too young to understand. I ask you if you have any questions about us. You always say something cute, so maybe it's too early. That's ok. I want you to be a little boy, for as long as I can have you that way. I want you to know I never wanted this. Also, that you were the best thing that could have ever happened to me. You gave me a reason to get up every day, and live. You still are that reason. Sometimes you may think that I am a little strict with you. Sometimes my patience is a little thin. I wasn't always like this Jake. I've just been through some rough times lately. Not having you and your mother in my life daily was tougher on me than anyone knows. I always tried not to show that to you. I didn't want to scare you. I want you to know that you were not the reason your mother and I stopped living together. In fact, you may be the only reason we were together as long as we were. But I love you both, with all my heart. There is nothing in this world that I care about more than the two of you. But you Jacob - You're my Robin. After all life's done to me and all I've been through, you are the youthful innocence and wide-eyed wonder that I lost a long time ago. That's why Batman always had a Robin. Just to remind him. Your absent Dad.

Apparently the child needs $40 shoes. Naturally, these shoes will become obsolete in a matter of months as the child outgrows them. I have never understood why any parent would choose expensive apparel for a child. It is foolish to pay so much money for such little utility. Yet, the ex is of the belief that her child needs lavish things, and now we owe her $20. My miserly ways are livid with this obligation; however, my husband committed to pay half prior to the purchase. Next time the child needs new shoes, we shall buy them.

I stood up for myself only once to the ex. It's not that I'm against standing up for myself, but I do pick my battles. Plus, I choose not to be around her when I can. She's just cantankerous, and I find that annoying.

My husband and I attended the middle school parent/teacher conference. It was fall, and we opted to go together and split up the eight classes so that we could see all of the instructors. I recall my parents doing this same thing, and it worked well for them. We arrived first to the school. Unsure of what the ex's plans were, we made our plans. There was nothing preventing her from seeing the instructors on her own. Divorced parents do that all the time and teachers are accustomed to dealing with this. I believe we were there for only a few minutes, and the ex came storming in.

I didn't expect her to immediately call my stepchild after parent/teacher conference and tell them how I was mean to her. How we got into a fight, and I was mean. Naturally, the stepchild took her side and wanted to discuss it in great detail with his father. One day my stepchild and I will discuss this, but I am purposefully waiting until adulthood.

I should also remind you that my stepchild takes their mother's side in everything. It's their dad's fault for everything wrong in the marriage and pending divorce with their mother. It's the public school's fault their mother was bored in high school and almost didn't graduate. It's the fault of their mother's past bosses that she has been laid off multiple times. It must suck to be her with everyone burdening her life so. *sarcasm*

These comments portray the complexity and difficulty found in relationships wherein ex-spouses and stepchildren are involved. These comments and others like it demonstrate the animosity that can mount in these relationships. As the conflict continues to brew, the children become further entrenched and, ultimately, they are the ones most negatively affected.

Myth Reconstruction and Implications

Hofferth et al. (2010) have maintained that improving the relationship between the present and absent parent serves as a critical task of postdivorce functioning. It is important so that each can begin a new life, it is important for the well-being of the children, and (according to Shafer et al., 2013) it facilitates the sustainability of the new stepfamily. Stepparents should accept that, as far as the children are concerned, the biological parent may always come first. However, mutual acceptance of the complementary contribution of both biological parents and stepparents can greatly contribute to stepfamily sustainability. Deal (2013) suggested that the new stepparent and residential custodial parent accept what they cannot change and recognize their own part in maintaining whatever conflict exists with the noncustodial parent. The driving concern has to be "what is best for the children?" rather than "how do I show that I am the better parent?" Throughout this adjustment period, relational expectations and role enactments remain unstable (Shafer et al., 2013). Nebulous role definitions, interactions between ex-spouses who are required to coparent, and the inclusion of the stepparent make it necessary to reauthor the myth.

Myth #1: Children Can Be Loyal Only to the Biological Parent, Not to the Stepparent

Myth Reauthoring

The introduction of a new stepparent is an addition to the number of adults who care about the children and are committed to their well-being. Joining the family does not represent a competition or an attempt to replace the biological parent.

Implications for Effective Ex-Spousal Relationships

The notion of parental loyalty cannot be confused with adult affiliation. While the residential parent and stepparent enjoy physical proximity, the nonresidential parent can remain as important to the children as he or she chooses and is able to consistently enact (Wolf, 2011). This is possible if past spousal hurts are relegated to the past and if both parents try to maintain a collaborative consistent parenting coalition (Gold, 2010). This, in turn, is possible if the adults constrain any criticism or concerns among themselves and never initiate such discussions within the hearing of the children or involve the children directly in any of these discussions.

Myth #2: Divorced Couples Cannot Agree on Anything

Myth Reauthoring

After a divorce, the disagreements that severed the marriage become irrelevant compared to the needs of the children. It is important that the former couple deal with the lingering emotional hurt of the divorce separately and that they do not allow the past to hinder their efforts to become effective, collaborative coparents.

Implications for Effective Ex-Spousal Relationships

Ex-spouses are challenged to work hard to respect the other parent and his or her household. The ideal relationship of separate but consistent parenting provides a sense of stability and security for the children, alleviates the residential parent from being the sole disciplinarian, and saves the nonresidential parent from acting solely as a "Disney" parent, whose only function is to entertain and not to do the work of actual parenting. Therefore, all matters pertaining to the discipline and care of the children must be addressed, negotiated, and settled amicably.

Myth #3: Divorced Couples Want the Ex-Spouse Out of the Children's Lives

Myth Reauthoring

The term *ex-spouse* denotes a clinging to an extinct relationship. A divorced couple should think of themselves as nonresidential coparents, and, for the sake of the children, they must cooperate to promote stability and constancy of affection and support in their lives, albeit in two different households.

Implications for Effective Ex-Spousal Relationships

It seems unfair to wield the affections and affiliations of the children as a weapon in postdivorce relationships. While there are instances where continued contact may be detrimental to the well-being of the children (e.g., an addicted or abusive parent), in most cases, any attempt to limit court-approved access and contact reflects lingering marital issues and is unfair to the ex-spouse or children. Wolf (2011) advised nonresidential parents to be as important to their children as they choose to be; they should have scheduled patterns of interaction (nightly for younger children or those coping with recent separation), and ongoing regular contact even if the children are not available or willing to talk at that moment. During those contacts, nonresidential parents can try to remain current with activities, accomplishments, interests, and friends. In addition, Wolf suggested that noncustodial parents send messages, newspaper articles, e-mails, and other communications to reassure the children of their continued affection and sincerity. Noncustodial parents must also learn how to communicate with the ex-spouse about the lives of the children. Their involvement will pay off down the road in the continued closeness with the children as they grow into adulthood.

Myth #4: The Stepparent Is Trying to "Replace" the Biological Parent

Myth Reauthoring

What each adult contributes to the health and welfare of each child is unique. One caring adult figure cannot "replace" another, as the emotional gifts and child's experience of each will be unique and honored. Moreover, any attempt to downgrade or demean the (step)parent will only generate pain, loyalty conflicts, and tension within the children.

Implications for Effective Ex-Spousal Relationships

As a biological parent, the nonresidential mother or father already possesses something the stepparent can never have: history with each child (Gold, 2010). This unique bond can serve as the foundation for ongoing connection between biologically linked family members. This history brings with it memories, traditions, rites of passage, and shared hobbies and interests to which the stepparent may add over time but can never replicate. One set of experiences between adult and child may augment the other but cannot replace or even duplicate them.

There is a ring of truth in the original myth, however: The nonresidential parent has been replaced, but as a spouse and not as a parent. It therefore becomes critical that the two roles be distinguished. The therapeutic work to resolve the spousal severing cannot be allowed to taint the ongoing parental and coparental roles. This process of "reimaging" an ex-spouse as only a collaborative coparent is probably the most challenging task facing each ex-spouse. However, its successful resolution is critically important not only for the sake of the children's well-being but also for the present and future emotional functioning of each adult.

Myth #5: All the Ex-Spouse Wants Is Financial Support

Myth Reauthoring

Financial support is critical for the well-being of the children. The non-custodial parent's ongoing contact and interest in their lives will pay the eventual dividends of a long-term healthy connection that now spans physical distance. Any possibility of increased participation in the lives of the children will be appreciated by them and will reinforce the parent's presence in their lives.

Implications for Effective Ex-Spousal Relationships

Divorce proceedings often end acrimoniously; the court's decisions on matters of finance may leave both parties dissatisfied. In addition, since the spending of child support monies is not monitored, the contributing ex-spouse may suspect financial mishandling on the part of the receiving spouse, and this may sour any discussions about ongoing financial arrangements. Divorced couples are encouraged to keep "business meetings" impersonal to avoid excessive conflict and to prepare a script to help both parties through negotiations; they should restrict their discussions to matters of parenting. Each party has legitimate concerns, and the agenda should focus on common ground rather than on proving who is right or wrong.

Issues of Cultural Diversity and Ex-Spouses

I have been unable to find any pertinent professional literature pertaining to the relationships of ex-spouses in African American and Hispanic stepfamilies, which suggests that focused attention is needed in these areas. Stewart (2007) reported that lesbian mothers seem to have a better relationship with their heterosexual ex-husbands than do heterosexual mothers with their gay ex-husbands. The quality of this coparenting collaboration seems a function of the former spouse's acceptance of the ex-spouse's sexual orientation. If the former spouse is still coping with feelings of hurt and betrayal, this residual emotional "baggage" will detract from their ability to collaboratively coparent with the gay or lesbian stepfamily. These issues become exacerbated if the ex-spouse has a moral opposition to homosexuality. In such instances, the conflict is based on such a basic disapproval of the sexual orientation of the ex-spouse that even appealing to the parent on behalf of the best interests of the children may prove unsuccessful.

Conclusion

The presence and significance of noncustodial parents in the stepfamily constellation cannot be denied; they contribute to the well-being or dysfunction of the children and the sustainability of the stepfamily unit (Gold & Adeyemi, 2013; Hofferth et al., 2010). As Gunnoe and Hetherington (2004) concluded, it is time for "parents, social scientists and legal professionals to consider anew the potentially influential roles of noncustodial parents in children's lives" (p. 562). Given the documented rate of stepfamily dissolutions, more attention needs to be directed toward the healthy inclusion of noncustodial parents within that family unit through assistance in resolving any residual animosity between the ex-spouses and the promotion of positive coparenting practices.

Resources

Anonymous. (n.d.). *Planning for remarriage.* American Psychological Association. Retrieved from http://www.apa.org/helpcenter/stepfamily.aspx

Common issues that remarrying adults need to resolve

Deal, R. L. (2004). *Dealing with a difficult ex-spouse: 10 Tips to help you cope.* Smart Stepfamilies. Retrieved from http://www.smartstepfamilies. com/view/116

Tips for establishing positive relationships between ex-spouses

Engel, M. (n.d.). *Suggestions for successful summer visitations.* National Stepfamily Resource Center. Retrieved from http://www.stepfamilies.info/articles/suggestions-for-successful-summer-visitations.php

Practical tips for residential and nonresidential spouses to facilitate healthy between-home living for children

Stile, S. (n.d.). *Dealing with your ex after divorce and setting boundaries.* Women's Divorce. Retrieved from http://www.womansdivorce.com/ex-after-divorce.html

Normative struggles and a series of positive interactional interventions

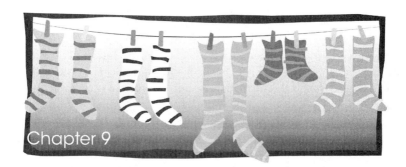

Chapter 9

Extended Stepfamily Constellations: Relationships With Stepgrandparents

As I was doing research for this book, I found to my surprise that nothing was available on stepgrandparenting. In this chapter, the term *stepgrandparent* refers to the biological parents of the stepparent, whose inclusion in the lives of the stepfamily occur as a result of its formation and who have little or no contact with the stepchildren prior to that family formation. Christensen and Smith (2002) observed that "current research is more focused on stepparent-stepchild issues with an omission of attention to extended relationships beyond the remarried family" (p. 119; Stewart, 2007). Yet grandparents are a valuable resource for families; the exposure of children to familial generations is generally seen as a positive thing.

The increase in the life span of grandparents has brought research attention on the relationships between grandparents and grandchildren (Attar-Schwartz, Buchanan, Tan, Flouri, & Griggs, 2009; Soliz, 2007). The growing numbers of stepfamilies in general plus the longer life span of the older generation means that children are likely to have grandparents in their lives; according to Christensen and Smith (2002), "95% of individuals will have at least one living grandparent by age 20" (p. 118). One remarriage by each biological parent can mean as many as four stepgrandparents added to a child's family network. Attar-Schwartz et al. (2009) claimed that the "number of individuals who will live their lives as part of three or four generational families is growing" (p. 67). According to the latest statistics, up to 33% of persons 65 years or older are stepgrandparents, and the numbers are growing rapidly (American Psychological Association, 2013; Attar-Schwatrz et al., 2009; Doyle, O'Dywer, & Timonen, 2010; Joanides, 2012). It is long overdue that attention be focused on their place in the new family constellation and on their needs and contributions.

Researchers have found that, for postdivorce single-parent families, biological grandparents have an important and positive role to play during this time of family transition (Christensen & Smith, 2002; Stewart, 2007). In a young person's changing world of parental relationships, grandparents may serve as the one stable relationship, especially if one of the biological parents is absent. Typically, the mother has been awarded custody of the children, and so the relationship with the paternal grandparents can provide an ongoing connection with the absent father. The biological grandparents may also function as intermediaries between the divorced spouses, keepers of the family history, and sources of economic and social support. Children from divorced families especially value their experiences with grandparents. Grandparents provide a sense of ongoing family. They have a special interest in their grandchildren, offering encouragement, a sympathetic ear, and (often) fun times.

After a divorce, a grandparent frequently becomes more important as caregiver, support person, or trusted adult. Many grandparents relish this role and become fearful of the impact of a new stepfamily on their relationship with their adult child and grandchildren (Stewart, 2007). While the role, place, and functioning of grandparents within the biological family evolved over the history of that family, stepgrandparenting occurs simultaneously with the marriage and involves children with different grandparenting histories. This anxiety may be founded in misperceptions regarding the issues of role ambiguity and lack of successful role models (Christensen & Smith, 2002). The benefits of the grandparent–grandchild relationship are known; one wonders whether the stepchild–stepgrandparent relationship is also enriching.

Importance of Stepgrandparent Connections

Carter and McGoldrick (2005b) asserted that "relationships with the grandparent's generation are critical in remarried families" (p. 431), which makes it all the more troubling that "the process of forming remarried family is inadequately understood" (p. 417). "Issues of boundaries and membership defy simple definition and our culture lacks any established patterns or rituals to help to handle the complex relationships of acquired family members" (p. 417). Social identity theory and social ecology (Soliz, 2007) suggest some possible benefits to be derived from the relationship.

Social identity theory addresses intragroup distinctions for the sake of common identity, such as "us" or "them" distinctions in stepfamilies. Because the kinship role is voluntary, stepchildren see stepgrandparents as resources in terms of social and personal roles, family activities, and emotional attachment. These dynamics seem dependent on the emotional investment of the stepgrandparents. They can tell childhood stories about the new stepparent, which helps to create a new family identity. This history allows the stepchildren to create a more complete picture of the stepparent apart from that singular stepparent role. Doyle et al. (2010) claimed that grandparents "play an important role in families that are undergoing stress or crisis" (p. 588). Those intergenerational connections have the potential to serve as a stabilizing force for parents, a catalyst for wider family cohesion, a focal point for family meetings, and (specific to stepfamilies) an invisible factor in the maintenance of the absent father's relationships with his children. These authors cited a 1990 study that found that closeness to paternal grandparents was associated with a greater capacity for behavioral adjustment in reconstituted families. This association can bridge imagined loyalty conflicts of the children and can balance any possible denigration of the noncustodial parent by the custodial parent. This relationship can also compensate for the son's lack of parenting skills if awarded custody, ease the period of adjustment for fathers, and serve as a support system and *kin-keeping* (an assurance of the continued emotional presence of the biological father despite his physical absence).

Social ecological theory posits that, to understand children's development, one must attend to their immediate connections, expanded to relationships beyond the family residence. Viewed as a "protective resource" (Attar-Schwartz et al., 2009, p. 73), grandparents can function as caregivers, playmates, advisors, and friends. Connections with grandparents can influence positive development (fewer emotional problems and more prosocial behavior) among adolescents either directly (through providing support) or indirectly by supporting the parents. Grandparents provide a consistent and active presence and, regardless of family structure and membership, ensure a "continuity of caregiving through multiple transitions" (p. 74). Doyle et al. (2010) stated that, in families undergoing stress or crisis, grandparents provide a stabilizing force for parents and a catalyst for wider family cohesion, a focal point for family meetings, and can serve as invisible factors in the maintenance of an absent father's relationships with his children. For the new stepgrandchildren, Soliz (2007) identified the following potential benefits offered by stepgrandparents: supportive sharing of family history, introducing the stepparent's family identity, transmitting values and beliefs, reinforcing cultural and ethnic or religious identity, supporting the stepfamily emotionally and financially, and acting as sounding boards during stressful events and family strife.

Although step relationships can be difficult to maneuver, a wealth of anecdotal evidence (including from stepgrandchildren) demonstrates how important they are. The active involvement of stepgrandparents has been found to be critical in facilitating one of the most vital tasks of the new stepfamily: "achieving a sense of shared family identity" (Soliz, 2007, p. 182). A 1989 study (cited in Stewart, 2007) established that most stepgrandchildren consider the stepgrandparent relationship important, express an eagerness for more contact with stepgrandparents, and maintain the relationship past high school.

Christensen and Smith (2002) discovered that "little research has been published on the relationship between step-grandchildren and stepgrandparents" (p. 130; Soliz, 2007). Perhaps the voluntary and transitory nature of this type of relationship based on the nuclear family "may not be extendable to relationships between stepgrandparents and stepgrandchildren" (p. 130). Because the subject is not addressed in the professional literature, family members have only social narratives to rely on for their understanding of these relational dynamics and how to facilitate positive connection between stepgrandchildren and stepgrandparents. The identification and reauthoring of these myths will provide knowledge and guidance for clinicians and family members.

Dominant Social Myths About Stepfamilies and Grandparents

The social myths described in the sections that follow illustrate some of the beliefs that stepgrandparents have. Each myth is described in this section; in a subsequent section, I demonstrate how each can be reauthored for effective stepgrandparenting.

Myth #1: The Role of a Grandparent Remains the Same Before and After a Divorce

This belief is based on the assumption of continued connection with the children. There has been a history, usually since the birth of the children, of relational dynamics. Birthdays, school events, sports, or cultural involvement all remain stable, as do the interactions with the grandparents around these nodal events in the children's lives. However, the belief seems to overlook the impact of the divorce of the biological parents, one of whom is the son or daughter of the grandparents; one cannot assume that the grandparents have remained aloof from any conflict or tension surrounding the divorce.

Myth #2: Grandparents Do Not Experience Loyalty Conflicts With the New Stepparent of Their Grandchildren

There is an optimistic hope that the introduction of a new spouse will be a smooth process, even though the new spouse is also replacing the role of one's own biological child as mother or father of the children. In this same rosy scenario, grandparents believe that one's own biological adult child will accept this addition of a new spouse and stepparent to his or her children; that any residual spousal conflicts or tensions have been amicably resolved; and that collaborative coparenting practices have been negotiated and established and are mutually enacted.

Myth #3: All the Grandparents Will Become Instant Friends

This seems founded in the assumption that "grandparenting" is a universal, or at least a cross-familial practice, around which roles of grandmother and grandfather, inclusion in the lives and events of the children, and the practice of family rituals are consensual. Even if the stepgrandparents and the biological grandparents share a commitment to the health and well-being of the children in the new stepfamily, the means by which they express these aims may not be shared. Grandparenting styles differ within the same culture, ethnic group, socioeconomic group, and religious or spiritual affiliation. Thus, the greater diversity carries with it the potential for misunderstanding, tension, and conflict between the grandparents.

Myth #4: Everyone's Traditions Will Be Integrated

Family traditions regarding the observance of birthdays, secular holidays, religious or spiritual activities, and summer holidays establish a sense of family cohesion and stability. Their celebration allows for family members to gather, usually with roles, functions, and expectations that have been established over time, as legitimate ways to honor the occasion. With step-families, this can be tricky. Take Thanksgiving as an example: A single day may not be long enough to accommodate the traditions of three or more sets of extended families. How this challenge is negotiated and resolved will either build closer family ties around this celebration or provoke ongoing conflict over whose traditions do (and do not) matter.

Myth #5: Grandparents Love Their Child's Stepchildren as Much as They Love Their Own Grandchildren

The legal addition of family members is not the same as emotional attachment to them. Even as stepparents struggle with establishing bonds of affection for their stepchildren, stepgrandparents are more challenged in their attempts to connect with the new stepgrandchildren. The history of connection cannot be discounted; the stepgrandchildren may not even be interested in having as deep a relationship with the grandparents as the biological grandchildren have. One may come to love one's stepgrandchildren, regardless of the step grandchild's affection for the step grandparent, but this is a slow and lengthy process and cannot be demanded or rushed.

Narratives: Members of Stepfamilies Describe Relationships With Grandparents

Just to be clear, these are grandparents of both my stepkids and my bio kid. I do get the impression that the grandparents fawned over the stepkids when they were babies, but they lived far away from them so it was not the everyday interactions [sic] like they have with this baby. Grandparents did move closer though, when the kids were toddlers. Grandma had a bunch of things saved from when SS and SD were babies that were handed down to my baby. There is a bit of bitterness because this baby actually uses the stuff Grandma buys, whereas BM used to throw out the stuff that Grandma bought for her kids. Anyway, the stepkids were pretty close to their grandparents, but with arrival of my baby (and, I guess, the fact that they will soon be teenagers), that relationship has cooled off tremendously. DH is just as peeved as I am about it, because we both think that the grandparents play a pivotal role in how smooth the transition is for the stepkids, with having a new baby around, especially since we actually live with them.

Here is an example: We come home after a day out on the weekend, with our guests in tow. Grandma is at the front door waiting, saying, "Where is my grandchild?" over and over. Everyone knows who she means, and I feel terribly sad for my stepkids, and embarrassed in front of my guests.

My MIL has never set eyes on our DS but she worships the ground that the kids walk on. It will be the same with the next one also. She made her choices in her relationship with DH & I by siding with BM and basically excluding DH from his children's lives at every chance. We have nothing to do with her anymore.

My FIL only asks about the boys (DS & SS), I rarely hear him even ask about SD and he does ask about my pregnancy but it's more about how he wonders why we are doing this again and am I crazy. I like the guy and sometimes it's funny but we'll see how he is when she arrives next week.

My folks of course adore DS to the point they moved to TX to be near him—the bonus was the day they told us, DS proceed to show them his Big Brother shirt. My mom almost died. They are cordial and thoughtful when it comes to SS, they include him when he is around. But he's not their grandchild. They've never met SD.

My parents don't treat my SS like they do the other grandkids (my brother's kids and mine/DH's kids). They get him a gift for Christmas, talk to him, take him places with my ds, kid around with him. . . . But they don't dote on him like they so the rest. And he doesn't expect it either. He knows if my kids are over that those are their grandparents and yeah, they'll get spoiled some. But he practically lives with his maternal grandparents and they spoil and dote over him. Also, my kids have my parents and in-laws. SS has my [in-laws], his mom's parents and his stepdad's parents too. And his grandparents have always spoiled him. He loves them so much. My parents don't feel the need to dote over him too because he gets that already and they don't try to be something they aren't to him. To him, they aren't grandparents, they are 'SM's parents.' the thing with us too is that SS hasn't been in our lives in 3 years. So right now it's like having a stranger over in a way. Plus he's never really wanted to get to know me or my family, so . . .

This is kind of a touchy subject in our home. The grandparents on both sides do make an effort in including all of the kids (I have 2, DH has 2). Christmas and birthday gifts always seem to be approximately even. However, my oldest son is favored by my parents over all the kids (even over my youngest). I think this is mainly because I was young (19) when he was born and while I lived on my own, they were very involved and spent lots of time with him while I was in school or working.

The kids are all older, no babies to contend with. Each set of kids had their own things they did with their grandparents before we blended our families. My parents love to take big vacations with my boys and often spend weeks or weekends at the lake. DH isn't comfortable with his kids going without him because his time is so limited as it is with his two. While I have mine the majority of the time so them spending a week or two with g-ma and g-pa is no big deal to me. Kids have spent a night or two here or there with their DH's parents but it's usually at their house and very limited because they are respectful about cutting into his time with the kids.

The hardest we've had to deal with was the end of this past school year. SD was "graduating" from 6th grade which is elementary school and at the same time BS14 was "graduating" from 8th grade and entering HS. SD's school had a graduation ceremony but BS's school did not (different school districts). We wanted to do something like go out to eat to celebrate SD's "graduation" but DH's mom turned it into a big "graduation" party at her home with gifts, etc. BS didn't like that she was getting all this attention and gifts when the rest of them were not. I tried to explain to him that he'll get a big graduation party in 4 years and that this was just to celebrate leaving elementary school where she'd spent the last 7+ years but he still wasn't thrilled about it and I can't say I blamed him!

When we became stepgrandparents the children were 2, 9, and 14. There were no other grandfathers in the picture, but there were two very active grandmothers and Carolyn would make three. Recognizing that we had not been around these children since birth and we had no idea what they liked to eat or what they liked to do, we decided to take it slowly. We were not going to try and make up for years of living in hours. We wanted to respect the other grandparents and let the children know that we were genuinely interested in a relationship with them.

The quotes suggest the diversity of experience as well as the preference of grandparents for their biological grandchildren over their stepgrandchildren. There also seems to be an acknowledgement of the presence of the numerous sets of grandparents but not of how to interact with or negotiate grandparenting practices.

Myth Reconstruction and Implications

Myth #1: The Role of a Grandparent Remains the Same Before and After a Divorce

Myth Reauthoring

This myth may hold true for the maternal grandparents. Their connections with the children through the custodial parent (more often than not, the mother) remain consistent. Even in this case, there may be an increased need for financial, emotional, or logistical support in the absence of the partner. For the paternal grandparents whose son has lost custody of the grandchildren, the role of grandparent is altered by the divorce. First, the grandparents may become the communication conduit between the grandchildren and absent biological father; they may want to maintain his emotional connection to the children in the face of his physical absence. If the children have a stepfather, the paternal grandparents must reconcile his presence as a new husband and secondary father figure with that of their son as the primary father figure.

Concerning the relationships with the stepgrandchildren, grandparenting must begin anew, regardless of the ages of the stepchildren; they simply lack shared life experiences and values. The relationship is completely new; it was probably not given much thought when the adults married and formed a stepfamily. The relationship should be optional, not something that is imposed by the stepgrandparents.

Implications for Effective Stepgrandparenting

If Myth #1 is reauthored, grandparents should adopt the following positions:

1. Accept a role as a side player, not the star of the show. No matter how central a grandparent is in the life of a grandchild, to the stepgrandchild, the new adult is a stranger. In addition, the stepparent is also a stranger and one in more immediate and ongoing contact in most situations. Stepgrandparents must seek ways to earn the relationship with the new child/ren while remaining integral in the lives of the biological grandchildren.
2. New parents mean new rules for all the children in the household. Support their expectations, find ways to praise them, and be slow to criticize.
3. Offer but do not demand a relationship, especially with older stepchildren. Just as biological grandchildren may distance themselves from their families during teen years as peers take priority, older children may be already shifting focus away from the new stepfamily and its inclusive grandparents toward young adult independence.
4. Stay out of family conflicts. There may be a tendency on the part of the stepgrandchild to seek allies in the "battles" with parents. However, while this intrusion on the part of the grandparent may have been tolerated in the nuclear family, in the stepfamily, the new stepparent would benefit in the establishment and confirmation of his/her parental role by the support of the grandparents on all sides.
5. Do not take sides, especially between the stepparent and the absent biological parent. Grandparents may feel that it is disloyal to accept the stepparent who has replaced their own child in the family. However, that new adult has been chosen by the custodial parent and, regardless of the older generation member's level of approval of that union, is therefore deserving of one's acceptance as a legitimate family member and contributing parental figure as determined by the three active parenting adults in the lives of the children.

Myth #2: Grandparents Do Not Experience Loyalty Conflicts With the New Stepparent of Their Grandchildren

Myth Reauthoring

It can be a challenge to accept the new stepparent who assumes the parental role that the grandparents' biological child once had. Often, the dissolution of a marriage is based more on spousal conflict and incompatibility than on parenting disagreements; severe parenting discord may have fueled the marital dissolution, but often, the cause of divorce is related to spousal dysfunctions. Ongoing positive parental relationships between biological adults and children tend to characterize better functioning stepfamilies.

Implications for Effective Stepgrandparenting

If Myth #2 is reauthored, grandparents should adopt the following positions:

1. Recognize that bringing two families together is very stressful. Do what you can to minimize the stress. The role of stepgrandparents must be supportive and inclusive rather than dominating and selective. The stepfamily unit is sufficiently challenged from within to create a new identity and accommodate the needs of new members without having to expand their attention, and disperse their emotional energies, to the older generation.

2. Do not express any residual anger or resentment you may still have toward the ex-in-laws or absent biological parent. The new stepspousal dyad is sufficiently fragile that it cannot handle extra emotional pressure or infusion. The new couple is confounded with the dual assumption of spousal and parental roles, tasks that are daunting when faced separately but potentially overwhelming when combined. These adults find themselves constantly challenged within their present environment and family and do not have the emotional resources to relive past hurts or imagined injustices from prior marriages. The boundary around past pain among the older generation is critical, especially around stepchildren who cannot understand the source of this anger, having not lived within that family unit. In addition, children may internalize this disapproval or pain and begin to assume that they are the cause of the stepgrandparent's suffering rather than, in actuality, innocent bystanders to this emotional turmoil.

Myth #3: All the Grandparents Will Become Instant Friends

Myth Reauthoring

Grandparents hold in common a concern for the well-being of their grandchildren, be those children biological or through marriage. In stepfamilies, however, there is a critical imbalance in terms of family history and connection between the biological and stepgrandparents. This disparity—in length of bonding, familiarity with each child, and proven "worthiness" as a grandparent in the eyes of each child—serves as an ongoing disadvantage to the stepgrandparent and may subordinate that relationship to that of the biological grandparents. However, equal grandparenting need not be equated with similar grandparenting. As stepfamily connections begin to form, it is critical that the relationship between grandparents be one of mutual respect and acceptance of difference as well as rejoicing at similarity. The emergence of personal friendships would be ideal if it occurs; more important is to honor the important role that each set of grandparents plays in the health of the stepfamily.

Implications for Effective Stepgrandparenting

If Myth #3 is reauthored, grandparents should adopt the following positions:

1. Reassure other sets of grandparents on everyone's continued involvement. Stepgrandparents may seem exciting to children, as their presence is newer than that of biological grandparents. In addition the stepgrandparents may seem to be overly eager to connect with

children and to be overly accommodating to their wishes. However, this stage of "infatuation" will pass; the more grandparents, the better. Each grandparent will hold a unique place in the heart of each child.

2. Just as the stepparent reassures the children of the ongoing connection with the noncustodial biological parent, grandparents should similarly reassure the children that they are not trying to replace or shut out their biological grandparents. Once again, the intent is inclusion of all and in the manner in which each grandparent wishes and each child accepts. Perceptions of competition in terms of time spent with and gifts given to the grandchildren may lead to tensions between grandparents about time spent with the children and what is offered. Grandparents should always remember that each has a right to love the grandchildren according to their capacity and emotional, financial, and other resources.

3. Cards, letters, e-mail, and Skype contact are all ways to maintain connection and validate statements of inclusion. Physical distance need not signal emotional distance, and care must be exercised within and between generations to ensure that all are included and informed, whatever the distance.

Myth #4: Everyone's Traditions Will Be Integrated

Myth Reauthoring

The centrality of family traditions confirms the family identity and establishes a consistent pattern of gathering and celebration. The practice of these rituals provides a social nexus around which family life can operate and toward which family members anticipate these shared festivities. Such get-togethers may include annual events such as birthdays, school holidays, and anniversaries, in addition to societally sanctioned occasions such as Thanksgiving, Kwanzaa, Christmas, Hanukkah, and Independence Day.

Each family establishes unique celebration "protocols" specific to each occasion, which include who participates, menus, commemorative rituals, and observances. Over the period of adjustment in first marriages, new couples determine how to accommodate family-of-origin expectations as they create their own practices. The expansion of the family-of-marriage to integrate a new stepparent and new grandparents with yet another set of holiday practices challenges the stepfamily to balance multiple sets of expectations and may generate more stress and tension rather than enjoyment.

Implications for Effective Stepgrandparenting

If Myth #4 is reauthored, grandparents should adopt the following positions:

1. Remember special events, for both biological family and stepfamily. While remembering itself may prove a challenge as nodal life events in previously unfamiliar persons are added to the list of those with whom grandparents are familiar, their inclusion is critical for the stepgrandchildren to be at least as recognized as the biological grandchildren.

2. Recognize that what works for one child might not work for others. While grandparents may enact time-honored traditions with grandchildren, there is no assurance that such observances are relevant to or appropriate for the new stepgrandchildren. Any imposition of old traditions on new family members may generate a sense that some traditions are being discounted and foster more alienation than affiliation between the generations. Therefore, it is up to the grandparents to discuss with the stepfamily how all traditions might be honored.

3. Family traditions in the stepfamily have to make allowances for the noncustodial parent, whose inclusion would indicate the continued importance of that adult in the lives of the children. The grandparents might be asked to negotiate that inclusion. Regardless of the grandparents' opinions of this individual, and that parent's periphery role in the day-to-day functioning of the stepfamily, his or her presence at family events confirms for the children the continued involvement, care, and support of the noncustodial parent.

Myth #5: Grandparents Love Their Child's Stepchildren as Much as They Love Their Own Grandchildren

Myth Reauthoring

In the stepfamily, there is little time for the "evolution" of affiliation between stepgrandparents and stepgrandchildren, as those connections are established simultaneously with the marriage. This immediacy of connection does not necessarily translate into "instant affection"; the assumption that this is possible places too much pressure on all concerned regarding a relationship that has yet to be established.

Implications for Effective Stepgrandparenting

If Myth #5 is reauthored, the grandparents should adopt the following behaviors:

1. Focus on the needs of the children, not your needs for the relationship. Allow the children to direct the pace and depth of connection and involvement. Invite a relationship but refrain from imposing it on the stepgrandchildren.

2. Allow affection (hugs, kisses, hand-holding) to develop slowly. The children's comfort with physical contact is a reflection of the degree of connection, trust, and affiliation each feels toward the stepgrandparent; the expression of those emotions through physical contact must be allowed to evolve with time, shared activity, and growing attachment.

3. Be supportive of their interests before you expect them to be interested in yours. With the lives of stepgrandchildren, literally an unknown in the early stages of stepfamily life, curiosity about who these children are as people, and their likes and dislikes, will establish a basis of a strong relationship. While the grandparents possess many interests that may intrigue the children, the novelty and tentativeness of the

new relationship is best offset by focus of attention on the interest and activities of the stepgrandchildren.

4. Be equal with gifts and give on special occasions rather than appearing to try to buy their affection. This notion seems self-evident. One cannot compensate for a lack of relational history through an outpouring of gifts. Establish a gift-giving pattern that seems acceptable to the parents and both biological and stepgrandchildren. Children are keenly observant to note discrepancies in such practices and begin to wonder about possible personal failings that might justify such imbalances of gifts. To prevent such distrust and suspicion, stepgrandparents need to act consistently so that all the children receive age- and event-appropriate attention through gifts.

5. Offer individual time to offset sibling or stepsibling competition for your attention. An increase in the number of grandchildren challenges the amount of time a grandparent can commit to any one child. While initially perhaps stepgrandchildren may feel more comfortable interacting with the stepgrandparent in the presence of other siblings, as the relationships blossom, individual time and shared activity may be sought. This individual time may be invited by either the stepgrandparent or stepgrandchild, with the grandparent remaining aware of needing to ensure that each child receives due attention based on age, interest, shared activity, and receptivity.

6. Let the stepgrandchildren choose the name by which they call you. They may already refer to biological grandparents by specific names and would feel disloyal to have to use the same identifier with the new stepgrandparents. With younger children, stepgrandparents can offer options from which they can select.

7. Recognize that stepgrandchildren may not take to you regardless of what you do. For whatever reason, invitations for a relationship may not be reciprocated. The stepgrandparent can explore with the parents possible understandings for any refusals and act on the parental insights. Continued invitations assure the stepgrandchild of the continued interest in connection without a demand for such association, allowing the child to respond as desire, interest, and familiarity build.

Issues of Cultural Diversity and Stepgrandparents

Stewart (2007) found that cross-generational connections appear more prevalent in Black than White stepfamilies. In the majority of these situations, the grandparent may be the homeowner, not the adult child or parent of the child or stepchild. About 25% of African American stepchildren live with grandparents as opposed to 7% of stepchildren who live with White grandparents. Fully 25% of African American grandmothers act as surrogate mothers as compared to 12% in White stepfamilies. More than 50% of all African American families include at least one stepgrandparent. These findings (which come from a single study) suggest the presence of stepgrandparents within the African

American stepfamilies, and they seem to play a more involved role in active parenting that do White stepgrandparents in their families. No studies are available on the role played by Latino stepgrandparents in the stepfamilies formed by their children.

The relationships formed by stepgrandparents and stepchildren of gay and lesbian parents seems to be divided into three categories (Stewart, 2007). Stepgrandparents who accept the gay or lesbian sexual identity of their child seem to generalize that acceptance to the stepgrandchildren; grandparents who do not accept that lifestyle generalize that disapproval to the stepgrandchildren. Some stepgrandparents "compartmentalize" their feelings: They do not accept the sexual orientation and lifestyle of the adults, but they honor the needs of the children for grandparenting.

Conclusion

As one stepgrandchild stated, "My life was already a juggling act. I didn't need any more complicated relationships." The issues implicit in this comment revolve around the complexity of the new step relationships and the child's confusion about how to navigate the increased number of relationships in his/her life. Stepgrandparents who are sensitive to the intricacies of the situation and respect each stepchild's needs and wishes about their relationship stand a good chance of developing a lifelong bond with the stepgrandchild. Perhaps the child's message is less "I don't want to" than "I cannot on my own." These relationships have positive benefits, but how to facilitate these bonds and their study has yet to be formalized. As Attar-Schwartz et al. (2009) asserted, "with the prevalence of stepfamilies, the role of the stepgrandparents in family functioning should receive more scholarly attention. Obviously, this is an area of stepfamily relationships 'ripe' for research".

Resources

Adcox, S. (n.d.). *Advice for stepgrandparents*. Retrieved from http://grandparents.about.com/od/grandparentingroles/a/Stepgrands.htm
   Practical tips for stepgrandparents in navigating stepfamily issues

Anonymous. (n.d.). *Step-grandparents*. First Things First. Retrieved from http://firstthings.org/step-grandparents
   Stepgrandparents tell what they learned about their roles

Denham, C. (1992). *The special tie: Grandparents*. National Stepfamily Resource Center. Retrieved from http://www.stepfamilies.info/articles/the-special-tie-grandparents.php
   Common concerns for grandparents and stepgrandparents

Summers, M. (n.d.). *Grandparents and stepgrandparents: How they can help*. National Stepfamily Resource Center. Retrieved from http://www.stepfamilies.info/articles/grandparents-and-stepgrandparents.php
   Suggestions on how the older generation can support stepfamily success

Chapter 10

Future Directions in the Study of Stepfamilies

In closing, it would seem beneficial to put what has been learned into a broader context. Two basic assumptions have shaped this book. The first assumption is that the number of stepfamilies is large and is likely to get even larger. Thus, clinicians should recognize the likelihood that their caseloads will include this family constellation, with its unique challenges (Skogrand, Davis, & Higginbotham, 2011). The second assumption is that the integration of narrative therapy with stepfamily knowledge is useful in light of the prevalence and potentially negative contributions of dominant social narratives to stepfamily success and sustainability. Each supposition will be briefly addressed.

Prevalence of Stepfamilies

Almost a decade ago, Michaels (2006) declared the stepfamily one of the most prevalent American family forms. More recently, Deal (2014) stated that 33% of all marriages form stepfamilies, and the Pew Report of 2011 claimed that about 96 million adults are part of step relationships; that 33% of all children will live in stepfamily home before age 18; and that 50% of all children will have a stepparent at some point in their lives. However, the low success rate for stepfamilies seems to substantiate the need for purposeful interventions that transcend self-help books and the paucity of current professional literature. Michaels (2006) commented that, within stepfamily couples, divorce occurs more quickly and at higher rates in re-marriages than in first marriage, and Deal (2014) claimed that only 33% of stepfamilies last until the passing of a spouse—in other words, more than 60% end in divorce. Moreover, the majority of stepfamilies dissolve during the formative years as marital and familial stress levels are measured at three times that of first marriages. Therefore, clinicians can expect greater numbers of stepfamilies on their caseload. In addition, school counselors need to be aware of this social phenomenon so that, in responding to the needs of the children, they can offer professional knowledge and intentional interventions. Moreover they can serve to legitimize the child's stress and normalize and support the process of adjustment.

Support for Narrative Therapy

Narrative therapy is a postmodern expression of cognitive–behavioral therapy, and it posits that current client dysfunction is based on a congruence of faulty belief and action and that primary clinical attention must be paid not to the overt behaviors or actions but rather to the covert assumptions and beliefs on which those actions are based. Attention only to the behaviors may expand one's interactional repertoire but does not address the justification for the current behaviors. Narrative therapy seeks to explore with the client the socially promoted beliefs that inspire what becomes personally and relationally unsatisfying experiences. The dismantling of those social narratives, their intentional reauthoring, and then the new behaviors that emerge from those new perspectives form a basic understanding of narrative therapy but are founded in the theorywide assumption of the existence of dominant social narratives specific to a given situation.

This book presents some of the social narratives and myths around differing stepfamily roles and suggests ways that narrative therapy can be used to rewrite these myths. Social narratives seem to exist for all stepfamily relations and dynamics; acceptance of the dominant social narratives did not predict stepfamily success, satisfaction, or sustainability. Michaels (2006) advised that programs must address cognitions (described as "unrealistic expectations," p. 142) before offering behavioral options, whereas Janzen, Harris, Jordan, and Franklin (2006) argued that stepfamily intervention programs should honor samples of societal myths utilize the "un-verifiability of myths" (p. 334) as a logical staring point from which to view the stepfamily dissatisfaction and dysfunction. Therefore, in both theory and practice, narrative theory has been validated as a means through which to analyze stepfamily functioning and as a credible intervention strategy through which to promote stepfamily success and satisfaction.

What Do We Now Know About Issues of Cultural Diversity and Stepfamily Life?

The professional literature identified four cultural groups about which significant scholarly attention had been directed: I decided to examine what has been published about African American, Hispanic, gay, and lesbian stepfamilies that would be important for clinicians. As even a cursory review of the chapters will reveal, the literature in these areas is sparse—not because these topics are not worthy of scholarly investigation but because few researchers have directed their attention to this topic in these groups. In addition, many other groups were not included in this book, including Asian American stepfamilies, Native American stepfamilies, and military stepfamilies.

The lack of research suggests avenues for researchers to explore, including the ways in which the experiences of culturally diverse stepfamilies mirror and diverge from the experiences described in this book. This book provides an adequate starting point, but much more work is needed. Narrative therapy of client coauthoring may yield a more accurate and applicable picture of stepfamily functioning; even if it is not generalizable to the entire cultural group, it will be relevant to some clients.

What Have We Yet to Learn?

Future Research

Falke and Larson (2007) conducted a meta-analysis of research (1980–2005) on stepfamily marriage. Success seemed affected by the roles of stepchildren, stepfamily complexity, emotional attachment to ex-spouse, serial marriage, and economic strain. They concluded that, for positive remarriage, couple consensus on the important topics, social support, and financial stability seemed critical. They also advocated qualitative study of reauthoring social narratives, and quantitative research emphasizing more longitudinal studies to identify stepfamilies that persist as compared to those that result in divorce.

Psychoeducational Interventions

Some family issues are unique to stepfamilies (Michaels, 2006). Citing previous studies (e.g., Visher & Visher, 1990, 1996), boundary ambiguity, conflicting loyalties, stepparent–stepchild boundaries, and the stepparent's disciplinary role seemed critical topics for the inclusion in preventive intervention with stepfamilies. The format is based on systems and social learning theory, focusing on a "normative-adaptive" approach seeking to promote positive dimensions of stepfamily perspective and interaction, as opposed to a deficit-comparison approach, which is more negatively focused and emphasizes distinctions between the stepfamily and first-marriage families. The format also honors the impact of adherence to dominant social narratives, which tend to prejudice family members against the very family constellation in which they exist. Unchecked, this recognition may prompt a merging worry about the future of the family, expressed in hopelessness, unhappiness, and growing alienation between the spouses. This is typically the point at which one or both partners consider divorce.

Published literature (Falke & Larson, 2007; Michaels, 2006; Skogrand, Dansie, Higginbotham, Davis, & Barrios-Bell, 2011; Skogrand, Davis, & Higginbotham, 2011; Skogrand, Torres, & Higgenbotham, 2010) attests to the success of psychoeducational interventions in terms of both facilitating identified stepfamily strengths and building a sense of normalization and cohesion among the participants. However, with 75% of stepfamilies not participating in these programs, perhaps the greatest challenge is how to advertise their efficacy, as is being noted, and their availability to increase stepfamily participation in what seem to be effective ways to promote the success of new stepfamilies.

Delivery of Clinical Service

Formalized and standardized assessment tools are available to validate the efficacy of the interventions described throughout this book. Given the multiple relationships that are all unfolding at the same time within the extended boundaries of the stepfamily and the intricacy of trying to separate these concerns for therapeutic attention (Janzen et al., 2006), consideration of assessment tools unique to the stepfamily experience would be a wise approach.

The Stepfamily Adjustment Scale (Crosbie-Burnett, 1989) consists of 45 questions seeking input from adolescents, parents, and stepparents. There are four scales to assess adolescents measuring: (a) psychological exclusion of stepparent and problems in stepparent–stepchild relationship, (b) problematic boundaries and relationships, (c) problems in biological parent–child relationship, and (d) the presence of child in executive system. For stepparents there are 40 questions divided into three scales measuring: (a) problems in stepparent–stepchild relationship, (b) dissatisfaction with roles of family members, and (c) lack of support from biological parent. The parent version (43 questions, 3 scales) measures (a) triangulation, exclusion of stepparent, and problematic boundaries; (b) lack of support and dissatisfaction with stepparent's role; and (c) problems in stepparent–stepchild relationship. There is a 4-point Likert-type scale applied to all questions.

The Stepparent–Stepchild Communication Scale (Barnes & Olson, 2003) asks 20 statements on 2 subscales: positive stepfamily communication and problems in stepfamily communication. Questions are scored on a Likert-type scale of 1–5. The instrument is designed to be completed by all members of the stepfamily. In addition, the literature review discovered two additional instruments with potential value: the Stepparent Relationship Index (Schrodt, 2006a) and the Stepfamily Life Index (Schrodt, 2006b).

These self-report surveys have not been evaluated in the Buros Mental Measurement Yearbook as of Summer 2014. Because I cannot include any test reviews and psychometric data, I am reluctant to include more than the names of these measures in this chapter for fear of appearing to endorse these assessment tools. The reader is advised to research each measure to confirm its validity, reliability, and usability. I note that no measure identified in the literature review included attention to the marital dyad.

Clinical Training and Supervision

Given the escalating demographic presence of stepfamilies, their inclusion in a clinical caseload carries a significant probability for all mental health service providers. This presence goes beyond mental health centers and private practice to school settings where the children of the stepfamily are expected to flourish and grow and whose development will require specialized intervention from school-based counselors, social workers, and other mental health professionals. These professionals need to be prepared with adequate knowledge of stepfamily evolution as distinct from first marriage, and the capacity to identify what is developmentally challenging versus pathological. These professionals also must approach each stepfamily member from a systemic perspective, because the stepfamily interaction can prove the greatest supportive and curative resource for the member who is currently in pain. Professionals also must consider knowledge of what is, and is not, known about the interaction of cultural diversity and stepfamily functioning and health. While stepfamily life in totality represents a statement of diversity within the wider constellation of families, attention to the nuances of stepfamily life and experience, as informed by culture, are critical aspects of joining with the family and legitimizing members' experiences. Finally, a clinician's investment in dominant narratives must be assessed to ensure that clinicians do not inadvertently impose negative social stereotypes on the families with whom they work. Mental health professionals who seek to intervene with stepfamilies must work beyond any personal experiences they may have as members of stepfamilies.

Conclusion

"It is difficult to visualize the future relative to the pace of the reconstituted family and how it will be viewed as an entity among other groups in society. Nevertheless, it is a family form that will continue to exist, and we must strive for the most effective way of understanding and dealing with these adults and children" (Janzen et al., 2006, p. 355).

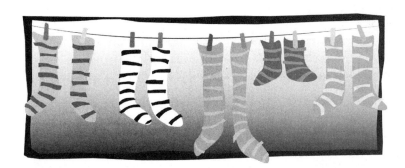

References

Adamsons, K., O'Brien, M., & Pasley, K. (2007). An ecological approach to father involvement in biological and stepfather families. *Fathering, 5*, 129–147.

Adler-Baeder, F., Robertson, A., & Schramm, D. G. (2010). Conceptual framework for marriage education program for stepfamily couples with considerations for socioeconomic context. *Marriage and Family Review, 46*, 300–322. doi:10.1080/01494929.2010.500531

Adler-Baeder, F., Russell, C., Kerpelman, J., Pittman, J., Ketring, S., Smith, T., Lucier-Greer, M., Bradford, A., & Stringer, K. (2010). Thriving in stepfamilies: Exploring competence and well-being among African American youth. *Journal of Adolescent Health, 46*, 396–398. doi: 10.1016/j.adohealth.2009.10.104

American Psychological Association. (2013). *Making stepfamilies work*. Retrieved from http://www.apa.org/helpcenter/stepfamily.aspx

Anonymous. (2006). *Wicked stepmothers: Fact or fiction*. Retrieved from http://www.siskiyous.edu/class/engl12/stepmom.htm

Attar-Schwartz, S., Tan, J., Buchanan, A., Flouri, E., & Griggs, J. (2009). Grandparenting and adolescent adjustment in two-parent biological, lone-parent, and step-families. *Journal of Family Psychology, 23*, 67–75. doi:10.1037/a0014383

Barnes, H., & Olson, D. H. (2003). *Parent–adolescent communication scale. Family inventories package*. Minneapolis, MN: Life Innovations.

Baxter, L. A., Braithwaite, D. O., & Nicholson, J. H. (1999). Turning points in the development of blended families. *Journal of Social and Personal Relationships, 16*, 291–313. doi: 10.1177/02654075991632002

Berger, L. M., Carlson, M. J., Bzostek, S. H., & Osborne, C. (2008). Parenting practices of resident fathers: The role of marital and biological ties. *Journal of Marriage and Family, 70*, 625–639.

Bernstein, A. C. (1997). Stepfamilies from siblings' perspectives. *Marriage and Family Review, 26,* 153–175.

Bigner, J. J. (2006). *Parent–child relations.* Upper Saddle River, NJ: Pearson.

Cadolle, S. (2000). *Being a parent, step-parent: Recomposition of the family,* Odile Jacob: Paris, France.

Carey, K. R. N. P. (2009). *The experiences of the African–American stepmother: An exploratory investigation* (Unpublished doctoral dissertation). Oakland University, Rochester, MI (UMI No. 3367680).

Carter, B., & McGoldrick, M. (2005a). Overview: The expanded family life cycle: Individuals, families and social perspectives. In B. Carter & M. McGoldrick (Eds.), *The expanded family life cycle: Individual, family and social perspectives* (3rd ed., pp. 1–27). Boston, MA: Allyn & Bacon.

Carter, B., & McGoldrick, M. (2005b). Remarried families. In B. Carter & M. McGoldrick (Eds.), *The expanded family life cycle: Individual, family and social perspectives* (3rd ed., pp. 417–435). Boston, MA: Allyn & Bacon.

Carter, B., McGoldrick, M., & Garcia-Preto, N. (2010). Overview: The life cycle in changing contexts. In B. Carter & M. McGoldrick (Eds.), *The expanded family life cycle: Individual, family and social perspectives* (3rd ed., pp. 1–19). Boston, MA: Allyn & Bacon.

Centers for Disease Control and Prevention. (1998, July 28). Births, marriages, divorces, and deaths for 1997. *Monthly Vital Statistics Report, 46,* no. 12. Retrieved from http://www.cdc.gov/nchs/data/mvsr/mv46_12.pdf

Cherlin, A. J. (1978). Remarriage as an incomplete institution. *American Journal of Sociology, 84,* 634–650.

Christensen, F. B., & Smith, T. A. (2002). What is happening to satisfaction and quality of relationships between step/grandparents and step/grandchildren? *Journal of Divorce & Remarriage, 37,* 117–133. doi:10.1300/JO87v37n01_07

Claxton-Oldfield, S., & O'Neil, S. (2007). Perceptions of gay and lesbian stepfamilies. *Journal of Divorce and Remarriage, 46,* 1–8. doi:10.1300/J087v46n03_01

Columbus, C. (Director). (1998). *Stepmom.* Burbank, CA: 1492 Pictures.

Council for Accreditation of Counseling and Related Educational Programs. (2015). *2016 standards.* Retrieved from http://www.cacrep.org/wp-content/uploads/2015/05/2016-CACREP-Standards.pdf

Craig, E. A., & Johnson, A. J. (2010). Role strain and online social support for childless stepmothers. *Journal of Social and Personal Relationships, 28,* 868–887. doi:10.1177/0265407510393055

Crosbie-Burnett, M. (1989). Application of family stress theory to remarriage: A model for assessing and helping stepfamilies. *Family Relations, 38,* 323–331.

Crosbie-Burnett, M., Lewis, E. A., Sullivan, S., Podolsky, J., deSouza, R. M., & Mitrani, V. (2005). Advancing theory through research: A case for extrusion in stepfamilies. In V. L. Bengston, A. C. Acock, K. R. Allen, P. Dilworth- Anderson, & D. M. Klein (Eds.), *Sourcebook of family theory and research* (pp. 213–238). Thousand Oaks, CA: Sage.

Crosbie-Burnett, M., & McClintic, K. M. (2000). Remarriage and recoupling: A stress perspective. In P. C. McHenry & S. J. Price (Eds.), *Family & change: Coping with stressful events and transitions* (pp. 303–332). Thousand Oaks, CA: Sage.

Cutrona, C. E., Russell, D. W., Burzette, R. G., Wesner, K. A., & Bryant, C. M. (2011). Predicting relationship stability among midlife African American couples. *Journal of Consulting and Clinical Psychology, 79*, 814–825. doi: 10.1037/a0025874

Dainton, M. (1993). The myths and misconceptions of the stepmother identity. *Family Relations, 42*, 93–98.

Deal, R. L. (2010). *Having an "ours" baby.* Retrieved from http://www.familylife.com/articles/topics/parenting/stepparents/stepfamily-living/having-an-ours-baby

Deal, R. (2012). *Remarriage and blended families.* Retrieved from http://www.focusonthefamily.com/marriage/marriage-challenges/remarriage-and-blended-families/the-smart-blended-marriage

Deal, R. L. (2013). *Dealing with a difficult ex-spouse: 10 tips to help you cope.* Retrieved from http://www.smartstepfamilies.com/view/dealing-with-a-difficult-ex-spouse

Deal, R. L. (2014). *Marriage, family, & stepfamily statistics.* Retrieved from http://www.smartstepfamilies.com/view/statistics

Deal, R. L., & Petherbridge, L. (2009). *The smart stepmom.* Minneapolis, MN: Bethany House.

Doodson, J. L. (2014). Understanding the factors related to stepmother anxiety: A qualitative approach. *Journal of Divorce & Remarriage, 55*, 645–667. doi: 10.1080/10502556.2014. 959111

Downs, K. J. M. (2003). Family commitment, role perceptions, social support, and mutual children in remarriage: A test of uncertainty reduction theory. *Journal of Divorce and Remarriage, 40*, 35–43. doi:10.1300/J087v40n01_03.

Doyle, M., O'Dywer, C., & Timonen, V. (2010). "How can you just cut off a whole side of the family and say move on?" The shaping of paternal grandparent–grandchild relationships following divorce or separation in the middle generation. *Family Relations, 59*, 587–598. doi:10.1111/jj.1741-3729.2010.00625.x

Erera, P. I., & Baum, N. (2009). Chat-room voices of divorced non-residential fathers. *Journal of Sociology and Social Welfare, 36*(2), 63–83.

Falke, S. I., & Larson, J. H. (2007). Premarital predictors of remarital quality: Implications for clinicians. *Contemporary Family Therapy, 29*, 9–23.

Favez, N., Widmer, E. D., Doan, M.-T., & Tissot, H. (2015, January). Coparenting in stepfamilies: Maternal promotion of family cohesiveness with partner and with father. *Journal of Child and Family Studies.* doi: 10.1007/s10826-015-0130-x

Felker, J. A., Fromme, D. K., Arnaut, G. L., & Stoll, B. M. (2002). A qualitative analysis of stepfamilies: The stepparent. *Journal of Divorce and Remarriage, 38*, 125–142.

Ferrer, M. (2012). *Stepping stones for stepfamilies: Lesson 2. Building a strong couple relationship.* Retrieved from http://edis.ifas.ufl.edu/fy033

Fletcher, J. B. (2010, October 29). And baby makes . . . six. *Remarriage Magazine.* Retrieved from http://remarriageworks.com/_blog/Articles/post/And_Baby_MakesSix/

Fogarty, K., & Evans, G. D. (2009). *The common roles of fathers: The five "Ps."* Retrieved from https://edis.ifas.ufl.edu/pdffiles/HE/HE14000.pdf

Ford, J. J., Nalbone, D. P., Wetchler, J. L., & Sutton, P. M. (2008). Fatherhood: How differentiation and identity status affect attachment to children. *The American Journal of Family Therapy, 36,* 284–299. doi:10.1080/01926180701647074

Forehand, R., Parent, J., Golub, A., & Reid, M. (2014, December). Male cohabiting partners as primary coparents in low-income Black stepfamilies. *Journal of Child and Family Studies.* doi: 10.1007/s10826-014-0091-5

Fredriksen-Goldsen, K. J., & Erera, P. I. (2003). Lesbian-headed stepfamilies. *Journal of Human Behavior in the Social Environment, 8,* 171–187. doi:10.1300/J137v8n02_11

Ganong, L. H., & Coleman, M. (1988). Do mutual children cement bonds in stepfamilies? *Journal of Marriage and the Family, 50,* 687–698.

Garneau, C. L., & Adler-Baeder, F. (2015). Changes in stepparents' coparenting and parenting following participation in a community-based relationship education program. *Family Process.* Advance online publication. doi:10.1111/famp.12133

Gately, N. J., Pike, L. T., & Murphy, P. T. (2006). An exploration of the impact of the family court process on "invisible" stepparents. *Journal of Divorce and Remarriage, 44,* 31–52.

Genesoni, L., & Tallandini, M. A. (2009). Men's psychological transition to fatherhood: An analysis of the literature, 1989–2008. *Birth, 36,* 305–317.

Gold, J. M. (2009). Stepparents and the law: Knowledge for counselors, guidelines for family members. *The Family Journal, 17,* 272–276. doi:10.1177/1066480709338287

Gold, J. M. (2010). Helping stepfathers "step away" from the role of "father": Directions for family intervention. *The Family Journal, 18,* 208–214. doi:10.1177/1066480710364498

Gold, J. M., & Adeyemi, O. (2013). Stepfathers and noncustodial fathers: Two men, one role. *The Family Journal, 21,* 99–104. doi: 10.1177/1066480712456829

Goldenberg, H., & Goldenberg, I. (2002). *Counseling today's families* (4th ed.). Pacific Grove, CA: Brooks/Cole.

Goldenberg, H., & Goldenberg, I. (2013). *Family therapy: An overview* (8th ed.). Belmont, CA: Brooks/Cole.

Gonzalez, C. (2012, January 24). Beat the wicked stepmother myth. *ParentLife.* Retrieved from http://blog.lifeway.com/parentlife/2012/01/24/beat-the-wicked-stepmother-myth/#.VU33_F4k_1o

Goodsell, T. L., Barrus, R. J., Meldrum, J. T., & Vargo, D. W. (2010). Fatherhood harmony: Polyphony, movement and subjectivity. *Fathering, 8,* 3–23. doi:10.3149/fth0801.3

Gosselin, J. (2010). Individual and family factors related to psychosocial adjustment in stepmother families with adolescents. *Journal of Divorce and Remarriage, 51,* 108–123. doi:10.1080/10502550903455174

Gosselin, J., & David, H. (2007). Risk and resilience factors linked with psychosocial adjustment of adolescents, stepparents and biological parents. *Journal of Divorce and Remarriage, 48*, 29–53.

Gunnoe, M. L., & Hetherington, E. M. (2004). Stepchildren's perceptions of noncustodial mothers and noncustodial fathers: Differences in socioemotional involvement and associations with adolescent adjustment problems. *Journal of Family Psychology, 18*, 555–563. doi:10.1037/70893-3200.18.4.555

Halford, K., Nicholson, J., & Sanders, M. (2007). Couple communication in stepfamilies. *Family Process, 46*, 471–483.

Harris, E. (2014, March 18). Grieving the gray divorce. *Chicago Tribune*. Retrieved from http://articles.chicagotribune.com/2014-03-18/features/sc-fam-0318-gray-divorce-20140318_1_adult-kids-divorcing-parents-adult-children

Higginbotham, B., & Agee, L. (2013). Endorsement of remarriage beliefs, spousal consistency and remarital adjustment. *Marriage & Family Review, 49*, 177–190. doi: 10.1080/01494929.2012.733325

Higginbotham, B., Davis, P., Smith, L., Dansie, L., Skogrand, & Beck, K. (2012). Stepfathers and stepfather education. *Journal of Divorce & Remarriage, 53*, 76–90. doi: 10.1080/10502556.2012.635972

Higher Education Act, 20 U.S.C. ch. 28 § 1001 et seq. (1965).

Hill, A. (2011, February 18). Fatherhood needs redefining, says UN report. *The Guardian*. http://www.theguardian.com/lifeandstyle/2011/feb/18/fatherhood-needs-redefining-un-study

Hofferth, S. L., & Anderson, K. G. (2003). Are all dads equal? Biology versus marriage as a basis for paternal investment. *Journal of Marriage and Family, 65*, 213–232. doi:10.1111/j.1741-3737.2003.00213.x

Hofferth, S. L., Forry, N. D., & Peters, H. E. (2010). Child support, father–child contact and preteens' involvement with nonresidential fathers: Racial/ethnic differences. *Journal of Family Economic Issues, 31*, 14–32. doi:10.1007/s10834-009-9172-9

Ihinger-Tallman, M., & Cooney, T. M. (2005). *Families in context: An introduction*. Oxford, UK: Oxford University Press.

Janzen, C., Harris, O., Jordan, C., & Franklin, C. (2006*). Family treatment: Evidence-based practice with populations at risk*. Belmont, CA: Thomson.

Jenkins, D. A. (2013). Boundary ambiguity in gay stepfamilies: Perspectives of gay biological fathers and their same-sex partners. *Journal of Divorce and Remarriage, 54*, 329–348.

Jensen, T. M., Lombardi, B. M., & Larson, H. H. (2015). Adult attachment and stepparenting issues: Couple relationship quality as a mediating factors. *Journal of Divorce & Remarriage, 56*, 80–94. doi: 10.1080/10502556.2014.972201

Joanides, C. (2012). *Challenges related to remarriage and stepfamily life*. Retrieved from http://www.goarch.org/archdiocese/departments/marriage/interfaith/attending-to-your-marriage/stepfamchall

Jones, A. C. (2003). Reconstructing the stepfamily: Old myths, new stories. *Social Work, 48*, 228–236.

Katz, R. (2010). *Stepmother sisterhood: The pros and cons of online support*. Retrieved from http://www.fsbmedia.com/article_display.php?article_id=975

Katz, R. (2011). *The plight of stepmoms on Mother's Day.* Retrieved from http://www.stepsforstepmothers.com

Kela. (2009, July 5). *Adding a new baby to your blended family.* Retrieved from http://www.todaysmodernfamily.com/index.php/1339

Kemp, G., Segal, J., & Robinson, L. (2013). *Step-parenting and blended families: How to bond with stepchildren and deal with stepfamily issues.* Retrieved from http://www.helpguide.org/articles/family-divorce/step-parenting-blended-families.htm

Kerns, D. (2009). *Stages of stepfamily development.* Retrieved from http://missourifamilies.org/features/divorcearticles/divorcefeature42.htm

King, V. (2009). Stepfamily formation: Implications for adolescent ties to mothers, nonresident fathers, and stepfathers. *Journal of Marriage and Family, 71,* 954–968.

King, V., Boyd, L. M., & Thorsen, M. L. (2015). Adolescents' perceptions of family belonging in stepfamilies. *Journal of Marriage and Family, 77,* 761–777. doi: 10.1111/jomf.12181

Kinniburgh-White, R., Cartwright, C., & Seymour, F. (2010). Young adults' narratives of relational development with stepfathers. *Journal of Social and Personal Relationships, 27,* 890–907. doi:10.1177/0265407510376252

Lambert, A. (2010). Stepparent family membership status. *Journal of Divorce and Remarriage, 51,* 428–440. doi:10.1080/10502556.2010.507128

Leland, J. (2014, September 12). Parenthood denied by the law. *New York Times.* Retrieved from http://nytimes.com/2014/09/14/nyregion/after-a-same-sex-couples-breakup-a-custody battle.html

Lewis, J. M., & Kreider, R. M. (2015). *Remarriage in the United States.* Retrieved from http://www.census.gov/hhes/socdemo/marriage

Long, L. L., & Young, M. E. (2007). *Counseling and therapy for couples* (2nd ed.). Belmont, CA: Thomson.

Lucier-Greer, M., Adler-Baeder, F., Ketring, S. A., Harcourt, K. T., & Smith, T. (2012). Comparing the experiences of couples in first marriages and remarriages in couple and relationship education. *Journal of Divorce & Remarriage, 53,* 55–75. doi: 10.1080/10502556.2012.635970

Lynch, J. M. (2000). Considerations of family structure and gender composition: The lesbian and gay stepfamily. *Journal of Homosexuality, 40,* 81–95.

Mahoney, M. M. (2006). Stepparents as third parties in relation to their stepchildren. *Family Law Quarterly, 40,* 81–108.

Malia, S. E. C. (2005). Balancing family members' interests regarding stepparent rights and obligations: A social policy challenge. *Family Relations, 54,* 298–319.

Martin-Uzzi, M., & Duval-Tsioles, D. (2013). The experience of remarried couples in blended families. *Journal of Divorce & Remarriage, 54,* 43–57. doi:10.1080/10502556.2012.743828

McGoldrick, M. (2005). Becoming a couple. In B. Carter & M. McGoldrick (Eds.), *The expanded family life cycle: Individual family and social perspectives* (3rd ed., pp. 231–248). New York, NY: Allyn & Bacon.

McGoldrick, M., & Carter, B. (2005). Remarried families. In B. Carter & M. McGoldrick (Eds.), *The expanded family life cycle: Individual family and social perspectives* (3rd ed., pp. 417–425). New York, NY: Allyn & Bacon.

McGoldrick, M., & Carter, B. (2011). Families transformed by the divorce cycle: Reconstituted, multinuclear, recoupled and remarried families. In M. McGoldrick, B. Carter, & N. Garcia-Preto (Eds.), *The expanded family life cycle* (4th ed., pp. 317–335). Boston, MA: Allyn & Bacon.

Michaels, M. l. (2006). Stepfamily enrichment program: A preventive intervention for remarried couples. *Journal for Specialists in Group Work, 31*, 135–152.

Moore, I. J. (Director). (1977–1981). *Eight is enough* [Television series]. Hollywood, CA: Lorimar Productions.

Morgan, A. (2000). *What is narrative therapy? An easy to read introduction.* Adelaide, Australia: Dulwich Center.

Murkoff, H., & Mazel, D. (2015). *What to expect when you're expecting* (4th ed.). New York, NY: Workman.

National Center for Fathering. (2009). *Fathering in America.* Washington, DC: Author.

Nichols, M. P. (2011). *The essentials of family therapy* (5th ed.). Boston, MA: Allyn & Bacon.

Olmstead, S. B., Futris, T. G., & Pasley, K. (2009). An exploration of married and divorced, nonresident men's perceptions and organizations of their father role identity. *Fathering, 7*, 249–268. doi:10.3149/fth0703.249

Pace, G. T., Shafer, K., Jensen, T. M., & Larson, J. H. (2015). Stepparenting issues and relationship quality: The role of clear communication. *Journal of Social Work, 15*, 24–44. doi: 10.1177/1468017313504508

Palkovitz, R. & Palm, G. (2009). Transitions with fathering. *Fathering, 7*, 3–22. doi: 10.3149/fth.0701.3

Papernow, P. (1993). *Becoming a stepfamily: Patterns of development in remarried families.* New York, NY: Taylor & Francis.

Papernow, P. (1999). *Step together: Patterns of development in stepfamilies.* Retrieved from www.steptogether.org/development.html

Parent, C., Saint-Jacques, M.-C., Beaudry, M., & Robitaille, C. (2007). Stepfather involvement in social interventions made by youth protection services in stepfamilies. *Child and Family Social Work, 12*, 229–238.

Parker, R. (2007). The effectiveness of marriage and relationship education programs. *Family Matters, 77*, 57–59.

Pettigrew, J. (2013). "I'll take what I can get": Identity development in the case of a stepfather. *Journal of Divorce and Remarriage, 54*, 25–42. doi:10.1080/10502556.2012.725360

Pew Research Center. (2011). *A portrait of stepfamilies.* Retrieved from http://www.pewsocialtrends.org/2011/01/13/a-portrait-of-stepfamilies

Phipps, W. D., & Vorster, C. (2015). Refiguring family therapy: Narrative therapy and beyond. *The Family Journal, 23*, 254–261. doi:10/1177/11664807155792978

Planitz, J. M., & Feeney, J. A. (2009). Are stepsiblings bad, stepmothers wicked, and stepfathers evil? An assessment of Australian stepfamily myths. *Journal of Family Studies, 15*, 82–97.

Plunkett, S. W., Williams, S. M., Schock, A. M., & Sands, T. (2007). Parenting and adolescent in Latino intact families, stepfather families, and single-mother families. *Journal of Divorce and Remarriage, 47*, 1–20. doi:10.1300/J087v47n03_01

Portrie, T., & Hill, N. R. (2005). Blended families: A critical review of the current research. *The Family Journal, 13*, 445–451.

Reck, K., Bigginbotham, B., Skogrand, L., & Davis, P. (2012). Facilitating stepfamily education for Latinos. *Marriage & Family Review, 48*, 170–187. doi:10.1080/01494929.2011.631729

Saint-Jacques, M-C., & Chamberland, C. (2000). When parents remake their lives. Regards adolescents on the family redesign. *Anthropology and companies, 24*, 115–131.

Saint-Jacques, M. C., Robitaille, C., Gadbout, E., Parnt, C. Drapeau, S., & Gagne, M. H. (2011). The processes distinguishing stable from unstable stepfamily couples: A qualitative analysis. *Family Relations, 60*, 545–561. doi:10.1111/j.1741-3729.2011.00668.x

Santos, A., Goncalves, M. M, & Matos, M. (2011). Innovative moments and poor outcome in narrative therapy. *Counseling and Psychotherapy Research, 11*, 129–139. doi: 10.1080/1473314093398153

Schenck, C. E., Braver, S. L., Wolchik, S. A., Saenz, D., Cookston, J. T., & Fabricius, W. V. (2009). Relations between mattering to step-and non-residential fathers and adolescent mental health. *Fathering, 7*, 70–90. doi:10.3149/fth.0701.70

Schmeeckle, M. (2007). Gender dynamics in stepfamilies: Adult stepchildren's views. *Journal of Marriage and the Family, 69*, 174–189.

Schramm, D. G., & Adler-Baeder, F. (2012). Marital quality for men and women in stepfamilies: Examining the role of economic pressure, common stressors and stepfamily-specific stressors. *Journal of Family Issues, 33*, 1373–1397. doi:10.1177/01925/3x11428126

Schrodt, P. (2006a). Development, validation and association with stepchildren's perceptions of stepparent communication, competence and closeness. *Journal of Social and Personal Relationships, 23*, 167–182. doi.10.1111/j.1475-6811.2006.0011.x

Schrodt, P. (2006b). Development and validation of the Stepfamily Life Index. *Journal of Social and Personal Relationships, 23*, 427–444. doi.10/1077/0265407506064210

Schrodt, P. (2006c). A typological examination of communication competence and mental health in stepchildren. *Communication Monographs, 73*, 309–333.

Schrodt, P. (2011). Stepparents' and nonresidential parents' relational satisfaction as a function of coparental communication in stepfamilies. *Journal of Social and Personal Relationships, 28*, 983–1004. doi:10.177/0265407510397990

Schrodt, P., Soliz, J., & Braithwaite, D. O. (2008). A social relations model of everyday talk and relational satisfaction in stepfamilies. *Communication Monographs, 75*, 190–217.

Schwartz, S. (Executive Producer). (1969–1974). *The Brady bunch* [Television series]. Los Angeles, CA: Paramount.

Shafer, K., Jensen, T. M., Pace, G. T., & Larson, J., H. (2013). Former spouse ties and postdivorce relationship quality: Relationship effort as a mediator. *Journal of Social Service Research, 39*, 629–645. doi:10.1080/01488376 .2013.834284

Shapiro, D. N., & Stewart, A. J. (2011). Parenting stress, perceived child regard, and depressive symptoms among stepmothers and biological mothers. *Family Relations, 60*, 533–544. doi:10.1111/j.1741-3729.2011.00665.x

Shapiro, D. N., & Stewart, A. J. (2012). Dyadic support in stepfamilies: Buffering against depressive symptoms among more and less experienced stepparents. *Journal of Family Psychology, 26*, 833–838. doi:10.1037/ a0029591

Skogrand, L., Dansie, L., Higginbotham, B. J., Davis, P., & Barrios-Bell, A. (2011). Benefits of stepfamily education: One-year post-program. *Marriage & Family Review, 47*, 149–163. doi:10.1080/01494929.2011.571634

Skogrand, L., Davis, P., & Higginbotham, B. (2011). Stepfamily education: A case study. *Contemporary Family Therapy, 33*, 61–70. doi:10.1007/ s10591-011-9141-y

Skogrand, L., Mendez, E., & Higginbotham, B. (2013). Stepfamily education: Case study of two lesbian couples. *Marriage & Family Review, 49*, 504–519. doi:10.1080/01494929.2013.772932

Skogrand, L., Torres, E., & Higgenbotham, B. J. (2010). Stepfamily education: Benefits of a group-formatted intervention. *The Family Journal, 18*, 234–240. doi:10.1177/1066480710372479

Soliz, J. (2007). Communicative predictors of a shared family identity: Comparison of grandchildren's perceptions of family-of-origin grandparents and stepgrandparents. *Journal of Family Communication, 7*, 177–194.

Spring, E. L. (2010). An outsider in my own house: Attachment injury in stepcouple relationships. *Journal of Marital and Family Therapy, 36*, 403–415.

Stanley, S. (2015, January 22). What is the divorce rate anyway? Around 42 percent, one scholar believes. *Family Studies*. Retrieved from http:// family-studies.org/what-is-the-divorce-rate-anyway-around-42-percent-one-scholar-believes/

Stewart, S. D. (2005a). Boundary ambiguity in stepfamilies. *Journal of Family Issues, 26*, 1002–1029.

Stewart, S. D. (2005b). How the birth of a child affects involvement with stepchildren. *Journal of Marriage and Family, 67*, 461–473.

Stewart, S. D. (2007). *Brave new stepfamilies: Diverse paths toward stepfamily living*. Thousand Oaks, CA; Sage.

Taylor, C., & Taylor, G. (2012). *Stepfamilies: What about the couple relationship?* Retrieved from http://www.smartstepfamilies.com/view/45

U.S. Census Bureau. (2000). *Family and living arrangements*. Washington, DC: Author.

U.S. Census Bureau. (2006). *Family and family statistics*. Washington, DC: Author.

U.S. Census Bureau. (2007). *American national survey: Married couples and unmarried partner households 2006*. Washington, DC: Author.

Van Eeden-Moorefield, B., Pasley, K., Crosbie-Burnett, M., & King, E. (2012). Explaining couple cohesion in different types of gay families. *Journal of Family Issues, 33*, 182–201. doi:10.1177/0192513X11418180

Visher, E. B., & Visher, J. S. (1990). Dynamics of successful stepfamilies. *Journal of Divorce and Remarriage, 14*, 3–12.

Visher, E., & Visher, J. (1996). *Therapy with stepparents.* New York, NY: Brunner/Mazel.

Visher, E., & Visher, J. (2003). The remarried family: Characteristics and interventions. In E. Visher and J. Visher (Eds), *Textbook of family and couples therapy: Clinical applications* (pp. 523–538). Washington, DC: American Psychiatric Publishing.

Visher, E. B., Visher, J. S., & Pasley, K. (1997). Stepfamily therapy from the clients' perspective. *Marriage & Family Review, 26*, 191–213.

White, L., & Gilbreth, J. G. (2001). When children have two fathers: Effects of relationships with stepfathers and noncustodial fathers on adolescent outcomes. *Journal of Marriage and Family, 63*, 155–167.

Wilkes, C., & Fromme, D. K. (2002). Stability and change in the experiences of parents, stepparents and adolescents in stepfamilies. *Journal of Divorce and Remarriage, 38*, 109–123.

Williams, N. R., & Kurtz, P. D. (2009). Narrative family interventions. In A. C. Kilpatrick & J. P. Holland (Eds.), *Working with families: An integrative model by level of need* (5th ed., pp. 174–195). Boston, MA: Allyn & Bacon.

Wolf, J. (2011). *Be an involved non-custodial parent.* Retrieved from http://singleparents.about.com/od/communication/tp/involved_noncustodial_parents.htm

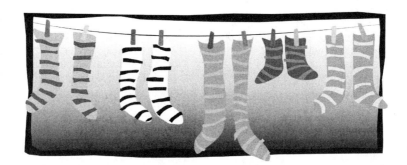

Index

(Continued)

L

Defiance
Rebellious
Exclusion
Different parenting (Household)